Mark M

THE ULTIMA1
BECOME THE PERFECT MAN:

UNIQUE SECRETS OF A FORMER CIA AGENT

Producer & International Distributor
eBookPro Publishing
www.ebook-pro.com

The Ultimate Way To Become The Perfect Man:
Unique Secrets of a Former CIA Agent
Mark McCoy

Contact: 11pridan@gmail.com
ISBN: 9781079893816

—— THE ——
ULTIMATE WAY
TO BECOME THE
PERFECT MAN

UNIQUE SECRETS OF A FORMER CIA AGENT

MARK MCCOY

CONTENTS

Introduction 7

Focus 9

Location, Timing, Observation 17

Your Car 25

My Umbrella 30

Big Mouth 37

There are Times... 45

And There are Times... 49

Take Care of Your Body 55

Dawn of a New Day 71

Man's Best Friend 75

Everything is Possible 77

Cheers! 85

A Well-Oiled Machine 95

Want to Undress? 105

Zorba or Charles 117

The Sixth Sense 125

Bond in London 131

Man al Dente 140

No Need 150

Twinklings of Understanding	157
Survival	162
Your Closest Friend	165
Steak-Steak	172
My Money's from the Bank...Yeah, Whatever	179
You, Me & the Car That's Following Us	189
Me!	194
End, Final, Terminal	200
OMG! I Don't Believe It!	205
Daddy-o	211
Codename Tehran	217
One Good Corner	220
Nightlife King	225
So, You're His Girlfriend?	229
You Can't Choose your Family	232
Monologue from the Vagina	235
The Peak of Excitement	239
Before We Part Ways	243
Decent. Cool. Generous.	247

INTRODUCTION

. . . .

Mark McCoy is a former senior agent at the CIA, America's intelligence organization. McCoy, fifty-seven years old, retired after thirty years of service, most of them as an operations officer. During his last years, he was mentor and personal educator to hundreds of senior agents all over the world. Many see McCoy as a spiritual teacher, a "Master of Life". According to McCoy, real professionalism comes from deep layers in the human psyche. Technical skill is necessary, it's true, but perfection only comes through systematic action on three fronts: man versus himself; man versus life; man versus others.

When McCoy began writing and publishing his teachings, he quickly gained millions of fans on five continents. McCoy speaks directly to men. The goal: to transform him into the ideal man. The means: a feminine worldview. McCoy believes that your wife is the glory of creation and that you should be worthy of her. Here, he comes to your aid.

A publisher in the United States once claimed that the day McCoy publishes a book, there will be no man who doesn't buy a copy for himself, and no woman that doesn't buy a copy for her man. Today is that day.

FOCUS

· · · · · · · · · ·

REMEMBER THAT WORD

Hey man.

You may be seventeen or thirty-seven. Single, married, divorced, widowed, straight, gay, bi, whatever you want. Maybe you have a girlfriend, maybe you have a wife, maybe you have a lover. Hey, maybe you have both a husband and a wife. Maybe you're a student, maybe a mechanic, maybe a broker on Wall Street. Maybe you're a lawyer, or maybe you need one. Maybe you have Attention Deficit Disorder, maybe you're in MENSA, the high IQ society. Maybe you're asexual, or maybe someone once set up a meeting with you just for a good blow job. It doesn't matter what type of man you are, and which features you came with – you're a man, in one of the many versions in which we appear.

Are you happy? What would make you happy? And what would make your partner happy? That's the problem. She wants you to be a real friend, a seductive lover, a great father to her children.

She wants you to spend time with her, but have a world of

your own. She wants you to be tough but romantic, she wants you to expand your horizons, but not your gut. She wants you to take her to see the world, but remember where you came from. She wants to go out, but wants to feel your presence at home.

She won't stop wanting. That's the source of the problem, and the magic, too. After you prove yourself in some areas, she'll want other things. That you'll be there at the birthing, that you won't be afraid to diaper the baby, that you'll be a good friend to your eldest child. That you stay in shape, don't smoke, and move up at work. That you can recommend a good book and watch *Orange is the New Black* with her. And after all that, after you've managed to find twenty-nine hours in a day, she'll want you to find one more hour for really great, creative sex. At least two different positions. She'll want all of her friends to want you, but for you to be hers. That you'll be a traditional type of guy and a symbol of new masculinity. Now, add anything else that you want to the list, and you'll see that life is just too short.

I took upon myself a mission: to help you be the perfect man. Insomuch as it is possible, of course. I'm going to deal with you. You're the subject. Take it seriously. Me, lightly. I'm here for you. I'm not the hero of this book. You're the hero. I've been the hero more than enough times. Aside from the times when I wasn't. We'll get to that too. I'm going to give you tools, knowledge and insight that will improve your abilities in everything that's connected to you. If you follow even *some* of the tips that I give you, your life is going to change. You're likely to become the man that every woman wants.

Tools, knowledge, insight. Believe me, you need them. You're missing them. It's not so much your fault as it is the fault of the world that you, me, and all men created. I get the impression that women have sources to draw knowledge from, while we men wander in the dark. Women's magazines cover almost everything, from pregnancy and birth to ski towns and shopping areas, from Japanese cooking to How to Advance Your Career in a Man's World. From Italian fashion to everything you wanted to know about sex. Raising children, raising dogs, raising husbands. We men have a few magazines on car mechanics and sports.

It turns out that we're to blame. Women have each other. They talk. They tell. They advise. They share. They admit faults and fears. They support each other. We men, we either keep quiet or we drone on and on. We can spend an entire night talking about who's making it to the Super Bowl and in the meantime, someone's making moves on our wives.

When was the last time you talked with a good friend about the fact that you're not attracted to your wife? When did you admit that you cum too fast? Did you ever tell someone that you never cum during a blow job? When did share your worries about money? When did you say to a friend, "I like you, I'm glad you exist"? When did you tell your girlfriend, "Listen, I'm not close with my father and it bothers me"?

Men don't take advantage of the source of information that's most available to them: themselves.

We men are suckers, and as with everything, we need to learn from women. Why are they the ones using moisturizer? Why are they indulging in massages and spa treatments? Why are they the only ones who know enough to buy comfortable underwear? Women who are friends can talk about everything and enjoy hour-long conversations because they talk about the things that really bother them. Men can only have deep conversations with strangers at a bar or with the bartender. Women talk with each other about their weaknesses in bed. They confess ("I don't have orgasms"), or admit to having fantasies and fetishes. Men report like journalists from the battlefield and in most cases, are not very objective. "It was mind-blowing." Yeah, sure. He'll never admit that he likes it when she spanks him.

Men live in secret, hiding from themselves and from others. It's dumb. There's no real closeness, just empty experiences (We won the game yesterday!" Who won? As though you yourself had actually played). Most men don't even have a normal handbag. Where do you put your phone, keys, wallet, cigarettes? You probably say: with her. Bad. Very bad. That's one part of a relationship I'm against. What is she? Your carrier pigeon? Either be independent or go out with your office assistant.

I know, I'm pissing you off. You think I'm making this up?

Let's see. You think that she suddenly disappeared. You stand like a jerk at a fountain in Rome, without keys, without a wallet, without anything. You can't even call her. Your cell phone is with her. And we're not even going to talk about how you're going to help her if she is suddenly in distress.

***

How am I going to succeed in giving you something? Who am I, anyway? My name is Mark McCoy, and I hope we're going to be friends.

I was born in the Bronx, New York. Dad was a boxer and Mom ran a catering company. After Dad was hurt in the ring, Mom made him retire and join her business. They bought out the other partners and worked hard in the fast food business. Dad forced me into the ring for a couple of years, until Mom talked some sense into him and convinced him to "leave the boy alone." I was a grown kid with a broken nose, two dislocated shoulders and stitches over my left eyebrow, but at least I knew how to protect myself.

Until I was twenty-eight, I spent a lot of time outside, on the street. On the ground floor, most of the time. It turned out that all of my jobs were on street level. I was a salesman in a video store, a security guard at a dance club, the manager of deliveries at a noodle joint and a pool lifeguard. At the request of a friend of my Dad, I took over as shift manager at a car wash. I moved up and became the manager. I liked watching people. Observing, examining. Every single person, their face, personality, secrets. No two people are identical. I saw thousands of people – every one of them and the scars of their lives. Their eyes, their rhythm, body language, hands. People who were happy and people who were nervous, angry, bitter, troubled. People who were full of confidence and people who were anxious.

I learned how to anticipate people's behavior from how they drove into the car wash. I wondered about people's personalities and how this suited their type of car. Everyone and their story. There are people whose story is ordinary, but a lie, and people whose story is extraordinary, but true. You can see a lot of people, but you don't really see them. I liked to observe. What does a man do while his car is being washed and waxed?

I understood that people come to the car wash and don't know what to do first: have a bite to eat or go into the car wash. Most of them decide to scarf down a hamburger, fill up, pass the time and then go out without washing the car.

Then I started a car wash business, small, my own.

Things went pretty well. The business grew. I bought the parking lot next to the car wash. I installed a new, more efficient machine. One weekend, I had an idea: Everyone who comes in for a rinse gets a hot dog. Straight to their car. What a deal. Water outside the car, the guy inside treats himself with some food. The moment he's finished eating, we clean his car from the crumbs. I became the biggest hot dog joint in the eastern United States.

There were days when I gave away eight hundred hot dogs. The only delay was due to the speed and capacity of the car wash machine. I developed a method that I called **five out of five** – which referred to the number of cars on the platform. The machine handled them like one huge car. I made it to one thousand seven hundred vehicles a day. People came by for the hot dogs. I went out in search for the perfect hot dog. I found a top-quality beef farm in Vermont. They developed a line of production especially for me. Six months later, I opened a snack bar on the side. The guy ate three hot dogs while his car went through the car wash. Things peaked on the weekend. The area was empty and entire families came from the suburbs. He came to wash the car; she came to feed the kids.

Hot wash – hot dog. No chairs, no tables. A huge round bar. Hot dogs, sauerkraut, beer, cola. Every day, some genius came by to give me advice. I knew that I shouldn't change a thing. Every week, I got new offers. Want to sell? Want a partner? I waited for the arrogant smart-ass to come. And he did. More correctly, *they* came. Four partners. I sold the business for a ridiculous amount of money. One added French fries. Another brought in newspapers and magazines. A third added waiters, and the last improvement was a fifty-cent surcharge on the hot dogs. Today, the business is closed.

Focus. Remember the word **focus**. That's the secret.

And then I ran over an old man. The judge found me completely innocent. One witness said that the guy just jumped into the road so he could be finished with this life and make it to heaven. But I took it hard. Why couldn't I avoid it, why didn't I see that there was something strange about the way he was standing on the curb? Where were my instincts? Trauma. I decided I needed a change. I moved to San Francisco, finished my bachelor's degree in psychology, started teaching karate and discovered the Gyro workout. We'll talk about it later. I started another degree but didn't finish. One day, two fellows showed up. They took me to an important meeting. To another world. My life changed that night. They presented themselves as representatives of an international company that sells expensive works of art to multimillionaires. I visited their offices and was impressed by the fact that they made no effort to hide the borderline gray area of their activity. The job they assigned to me was director in charge of Europe, a position that required special and prolonged training. I agreed. I passed a series of thorough and particularly exhausting tests. After an interesting, long and grueling journey, I discovered that I had been accepted by the CIA.

Sons of bitches. But I owe them a lot. I received training there for survival and for the art of life. The initiation period lasted for two years. Two intense, fascinating, formative years. Slowly, I started getting into the work. I traveled the world and saw a lot. Mostly, I saw that you need to see.

I asked you to take me lightly, but not just me. I want you to take everything lightly. Be more flexible. With yourself and with life. When there's a problem, coping with it sometimes is more problematic than the problem itself. Let's say you invite a date to a show. Second date. At the entrance to the theater, you discover that the tickets are lost. They don't let you in. Most men get dragged into thoughts and behavior that make the embarrassment even greater. It can't be, this never happens to me, what an idiot I am, and so on. I suggest you smile, give her a little hug and take her to the best bar in town. At the bar, after the second drink, you'll see that she's forgotten entirely about the show and admires you for being cool. The only question on her mind is her place or yours.

By the way, I would have been able to get into the show, and in the future, so will you. But one thing at a time. Let's start at the beginning. Come on, after you.

LOCATION, TIMING, OBSERVATION

···

THAT'S ALL IT TAKES

To be a CIA recruiting officer, you need to be a trickster, a survivor; sharp-eyed, bold, charming. A man of men and of shadows. You train in diverse areas. Not just in how to use a gun. That's obvious. You learn how to dress, charm a woman, enter a hotel room without a key, survive in a strange city, disappear without help, build a cover story and also – though it's unpleasant to admit – cause damage without leaving a trace. On the one hand, you need to have nerves of steel, be considerate, calculated and restrained; on the other hand, you must be creative, able to improvise, agile and quick at making decisions. You need to have a sixth sense at all times.

"I've got this feeling…" isn't just something we say. You need to be careful without ever tiring of being careful. If you ask me, anyone behind you is following you. You need an excellent memory, the ability to know where you are and how to navigate (everything is relative, but this was my weakness). You need excellent physical fitness and mental resistance. There is no end to the skills you need to develop

and the knowledge you need to have handy. You need to be an excellent driver, understand food, know different cultures and customs. You must know the human soul and understand how to silence it.

You need to be charismatic. People who don't know you need to act according to your manipulations. For example, take this exercise that students in the course are required to do: You must – now and quickly – find someone who will lend you their cell phone. Foreign country, different language, you look different. Who will you turn to? How much time will it take? Will you draw attention to yourself? Create suspicion? You're expected to succeed on your first try, within forty-five seconds. Afterwards, you need three more successful attempts.

This little exercise is just the tip of the iceberg. What will tempt people? What will change their minds? What will cause them to cheat? Betray you? When will you be able to trust someone? When must you avoid risks? How can you manipulate people and get what you want? How can you get people to trust you? To become a leader? The way I see it, everything depends on three things:

1. Location
2. Timing
3. Observation

LOCATION

Think about things that are completely different from each other. Judo, a passing car, breaking into a compound, building a house. In each and every one of them, location means advantage, control. Ancient rulers who chose where to build their fortresses, a lion preying on a doe by the shore, a rich man interested in buying a house, you looking to rent an office. What do all of these things have in common?

Often, timing is also important. Within a few days, the owner of a new café will find his favorite table where he sits and runs the business. I'll go into the café and be able to tell you where that table is within fifteen seconds. It's a matter of skill. Born and acquired. And there's more rationality to location. In an elevator, airplane, in choosing which line to stand in, where you sit in the theater.

Location is also a mystical matter. Things are not always under your control. A car swerves onto the sidewalk, a bullet is accidentally shot, a bouquet of flowers is thrown by the bride. Who will be hit by lightning? Early understanding and analysis are important. A striker can't know for certain that the ball from a corner kick will land on his head, but he can certainly increase the chance that it happens. The more elements in the equation and the less time you have to decide, the more skill you need to get the precise answer. Would you prefer to sit with your back to the door, or your face to the door but the sun in your eyes? Having sun in your eyes is temporary. You can wear sunglasses or a hat with a visor until the sun sets. A door at your back is a fixed and final fact.

A stewardess leaves the first-class kitchen with hot coffee. Who is more likely to have coffee spilt on them, the passenger in the first or second row? Clearly, the exit is the state of change, so it seems the stewardess will be less focused here. From this, it can be understood that the first row is prone to trouble. However, if the stewardess slips on her way to the first-row passenger, there's a chance that, in her attempt to recover, the first row will be saved, and the unavoidable collapse will occur at the second row. Of course, all of this drama could also happen in the sixth row. I just want you to start paying attention to detail.

A propos airplanes and the art of location, some airlines place security personnel on every flight. They sit in the same seats every time. It's not a coincidence. Someone explored the issue and reached the conclusion that this was the right place for the job. He was right, of course. It's the place I want for myself. But it's always taken. Always.

TIMING

This is no less important. Everything rises and falls in a decisive moment, the fraction of a second after which you might be burned. Any leopard can come within three hundred yards of any deer. The trick is for the leopard to get as close as possible before it starts its assault, a moment before the deer discovers it and tries to escape.

Anyone can trick anyone. The question is how far you can go before you're caught. A figure sits with his back to you; you approach softly on a wooden floor. The closer you get, the greater your chance of hitting him. The floorboards are old and dry. If you keep approaching, you may make a sound. Maybe he'll sense that something isn't quite right behind him. Maybe he also has a sixth sense. Chances are, he does. Which one of you will have the ability to know when one more moment is too late?

OBSERVATION

Unlike vision, observation contains two other elements: thought and drawing conclusions. The man in front of you is a resort manager in Thailand. He looks to be in his forties, tanned, fairly muscular but already developing a gut. He speaks English well. If you observe carefully, you'll see: the back of his neck is carved by deep sun lines; his hands are not the hands of a clerk, nor are they the hands of a farmer; his shoulders are not equal in height (the left one droops slightly); he wears safari pants with a belt; there are sunglasses hanging around his neck; on his left wrist, a Seiko watch; in his right hand, the business section from today's paper; it's eleven o'clock in the morning and he's clean shaven, with a few bristles under his nose. He socializes with some of the guests, doesn't really motivate the staff. At his temples, close to his hairline, there's a narrow strip of light skin. You've never seen him use a mobile device. And so on.

Now I'll tell you what I think: This man is easily seduced. Looking for opportunities. Unconnected and uncommitted. This is his first job as a resort manager, probably his last. Born into a middle-class family, Australian or maybe British. Moved around a bit as a child because of his parents' work. They must have divorced. Used to play tennis. Didn't try too hard. A bit lazy. Became a tennis instructor. Had a few good years. Knows how to connect with people and likes befriending his superiors. Important for him to look good, but not a perfectionist. Began drinking at night. Probably whiskey. Gained weight over the past two years. Discovered the delights of life. Wants money. Feels as though he's wasted years of his life, and now's his chance. Prefers nights to mornings. Had a haircut this week. Has problems with women. Doesn't have one right now. I wouldn't trust him.

Seems a bit too much? I won't go into the entire analysis. I'll just say one thing: You can spot significant weight change by examining the location of a belt hole. A hole that was used regularly is wider, and followed by a trace of the groove that was left by the clasp. When someone loses weight, the wider hole appears before the new hole; when someone gains wait, the wider hold is behind it. Observation is the basis for every decision.

One of the stages in agent training is catching pickpockets. It's our contribution to the local police force. The trainers put you in a crowded subway line that suffers from petty crime. You have to spot the person who just pickpocketed someone and make a sign to an undercover cop so they can catch the thief red-handed. You're measured by your ability to assess and locate.

I've never understood how pickpockets don't realize that if they wear sunglasses when they read the newspaper, I'll spot them in a second.

YOUR CAR

. . . .

CITY OF REFUGE

Ever since I had my old Pontiac with the hole around the antenna, I've understood that a car is much more than a car. It's a city of refuge. Seats, heating, music, a phone, GPS, glove compartment, mirror – where else do you have so much comfort, so much privacy, such control? Try to adopt the belief that your car is your mobile rescue station. Anytime, anywhere.

Your vehicle is you. Not in the eyes of those around you; in your eyes. Every detective, every mafia man, every character in a movie was close to the car that represented him. Just look how right a pickup was for Mel Gibson. So he could take his dog, go to the mountains, and threaten to kill himself with a gun. Imagine Gibson in a Ford Fiesta. No way.

One time, when I was on a mission in Beirut, we were looking for a car that wouldn't stand out. In the end we took a '69 Mercedes and installed a new eight-cylinder engine. It looked like a pile of junk, but we knew we could rely on it.

PREPARATION

It's true that, as someone who has spent many a night in his car, I may be exaggerating a bit, but a car is definitely something that can be used as an emergency storage room. First of all, stick a duplicate key on the underside of the car. There are tiny magnetic boxes designed exactly for this. Sound silly? Let's say you go to a movie. Just as you arrive at the car, your keys slip out of your hand, straight into the sewer. Your date thinks the situation is lost, that you're a moron, an unlucky bastard. Don't let her jump to conclusions. Go to the car nonchalantly, reach under the bumper, take out the duplicate key, and start the car which *also* contains a spare key to your apartment. You come out looking like a magician, a king, a man, and she'll never forget it.

Keep a small suitcase in the trunk of your car. Put a spare key to your apartment in it. Put toiletries, underwear, a T-shirt, socks, an old leather jacket. In the glove compartment, I want you to have a few items handy at all times: Tylenol, antihistamines for sudden allergic reactions, gloves. You can also keep some Viagra here for all I care, but you must remember one thing: aspirin. If you feel bad suddenly or think you're having a heart attack, aspirin can save your life. It gives you about two hours to make it to a hospital. No heart attack, no problem, but there's aspirin in the glove compartment.

No less critical: pills to stop diarrhea. Every secret agent in the world keeps aspirin and a pill to stop diarrhea in his wallet. You've been watching a suspect for an entire night, and just when he leaves his apartment, you have a bout of diarrhea. By the way, just then, because of the sudden excitement, that's exactly what happens. If you go for a walk along the beach with her on your first date and you get diarrhea – not so fun.

Go to the pharmacy and get yourself an EpiPen (you know, those needles that you self-inject into your thigh) against poison, nerve gas, bee stings and severe allergies. It's true, you're not a secret agent, but it's a good idea and can save your life. Assassination attempts are not uncommon in the world of espionage, and there are cases of mistaken identity. It could happen to you. Our agent in Cambodia was attacked by a swarm of bees and immediately developed an allergic reaction that was expressed in suffocation. He injected himself with his EpiPen and was saved.

Young children suffer from stridor. The result is dramatic stenosis of the windpipe. An injection prevents suffocation.

Hide a bit of money in your car too, local currency, or foreign currency if you are abroad. You can't always find an ATM when you need one. What I'm trying to say is, don't rely on one. It's true, someone could steal your car, but you don't have anything of real value in it anyway, just some equipment for moments of truth. Needless to say, it's best if you know how to change a tire, and everything else that has to do with that. Don't be lazy; give the whole thing a try on some free weekend. You don't want to go out looking for the spare wheel on a stormy night. Don't get stuck without gas. Leave the humiliations to someone else.

If you don't have a cell phone installed in your car and only have one mobile device, make sure you keep a spare device in the car. It's nighttime, late, you discover that you've lost your phone. Don't rely on the mercy of someone on the street. Take a photo of your car papers and put them in the suitcase. You don't have your license, but at least you have a photograph. It could save you a nighttime trip to the local sheriff's office. The same logic is behind packing toiletries, a razor, a change of clothes—you never know when you might have a fling. This way, you have everything you need in your car, even after-shave. You know the saying "A man's home is his castle." Well, I say, "A man's car is his embassy." Secret apartment, weapons, communication and support center. By the way, I also have a jar of instant coffee in the car. Press the bottom of the jar, wait five seconds, and voila – hot coffee. The day will come, probably at night, when I'll use it.

DRIVING

When it comes to using the car, let me give you some advice: Take a driving course. I recommend rally driving and a few lessons on an ice rink. This is much more important than another trip to London or a lazy week in Thailand. A few facts:

- On a winding, smooth road, one where you usually drive no more than thirty miles an hour, you'll be able to drive up to fifty miles an hour if not more.
- If you find yourself in a ditch after skidding off the road, you'll continue on your way to Venice as if nothing happened.
- On a frozen lake in Lapland, you do a lap in ten, eleven minutes. A professional rally driver does it in six. I do it in seven, eight. A few lessons, a few sessions, you can too.

Before you take a driving course, you should learn some driving secrets. First of all, you need to know whether you're driving a vehicle with front or rear-wheel drive. In front-wheel drive, the motor is connected to and powers the front wheels. In rear-wheel drive, the motor is connected and powers the rear wheels. Classic European vehicles like BMW and Mercedes have rear-wheel drive; Japanese cars like Toyota and Mazda have front-wheel drive. Rear-wheel drive vehicles tend to oversteer. This means that when you're going into a turn, the rear part of the car seems to want to push straight forward, causing the front part of the car to go too far into the turn and risk spinning out. A vehicle with front-wheel drive has the opposite problem. It has sub-steering, which means the front part of the car slides away from the direction of the turn.

The treatment for these two problems is the opposite of each other. That's why for amateur drivers, front-wheel drive is preferable. Avoiding the skid is done with a driver's natural instinct. Experienced drivers and rally drivers prefer rear-wheel drive because it allows for a controlled skid. Amidst all of this, remember that the distribution of the car's weight over its wheels is very important. When a car accelerates, it rises slightly at the front which means there is less weight on the front wheels. When braking, the car goes down a bit at the front, which means there is less weight on the rear wheels. This basic law of physics directly affects the car's grip on the road.

Take a course, you'll learn and understand. Not only is it fun, but it gives you some important experience. Remember this simple fact: You'll never be able to hire a skilled driver. Worse than that, if you don't learn, you'll never be able to get away from one.

MY UMBRELLA

....

A STORY WITHOUT A MORAL, MAYBE WITH

She was my operations partner. Daria. I broke a basic rule. I fell in love in her. I broke an even more basic rule. I didn't report it. Her code name was Umbrella. I needed her when it was sunny, too.

She was a few years younger than me, a graduate from a prestigious university in the east. Brunette, green eyes, one hundred and thirty pounds, five feet seven inches tall. Liked skiing and guns. Her father had been in the army in a senior position. Eliminated from a navy pilot course just before the end. He was fluent in five languages. Tough face, strong handshake, soft soul.

We started off on the wrong foot. She lost a target (the person she was tracking). I was in charge of the front command room. During the investigation, I was cool and cynical. She argued that more pressure in the tracking would cause her to be exposed. I said I wasn't sure that would be such a loss. Hurried and stupid. She refused to accept my apology, justifiably.

Years later, she was assigned to be my partner. We spent weeks together. Trained in source security (a method for preventing source exposure), geolocation (location discovery using technology), situations and reactions (action scenario analysis). We passed our tests with the highest grades. Our assessor snooped to see if I didn't know her a bit too well. I said no. At the time, it was true.

Our first mission was in Spain. We arrived as a couple on vacation. I was transfixed by how she looked in her outfit. We stayed in the same hotel room. We were ordered to follow a meeting between two Iranian agents and two German arms dealers. There was a well-founded suspicion that the Germans were transferring anti-aircraft missiles to a country that supported terrorism. The Israeli Mossad had passed on the information. I was worried that there would be Mossad agents in the hotel too, and that they would interfere with our surveillance.

At night, we went for a stroll to gather more preoperative information. We spotted the Germans, identified their rental car, and attached a tracking device to it that transmits location data. At breakfast the next morning, I stayed in the room and Daria was supposed to go downstairs with tourist maps of the area. The Germans began talking with her. Superficial familiarity. Toward evening, they invited her to a drink at the bar. She sent me a message and I came downstairs. I joined them. They were in Spain as representatives of a company that markets adventure tours for Germans (a classic agent cover story which allows them to go on tours, "get lost" and ask lots of questions). I thought one of them was flirting with her. She giggled and let him touch her to his heart's content.

Back in our room, I told her that I thought there had been excessive contact. She asked if I was jealous. I told her that

I wasn't really her boyfriend. She started exercising in the room. I pretended to be absorbed in the news. Her sweaty shirt distracted me from the screen. Her nipples were clearly visible. Her breasts bounced at different rhythms. She was absorbed in the music from her headphones. When she moved on to sit-ups, she asked if I could hold her legs. Silly and reckless. Maybe not. I got up, sat on the carpet, and held her feet. She folded herself up and down, over and over again. Her shirt stuck to her chest. My breath stuck in my throat.

"Are you going to shave?" She asked, panting. "Why, should I?" I answered. "I think so," she said. "We sound like a couple," I said. "We're not?!" she wondered. "Could we be?" I snapped back. "If you didn't work at the office," she answered. A surprise. What did she mean, I wondered. "Who would be with the children now?" she added, reading my thoughts. "Do you want children?" I asked. Silence. In response, I leaned toward her, she was sweaty and sexier than ever, and put my lips closer to hers. We were drawn passionately. In a moment, she took charge. I experienced a moment I didn't want to end. A warm, open, intensive moment. Comfort, that's the word.

My loneliness vanished as though it had never been there. I felt as though I was a part of something. To someone. I wanted to live. I was afraid it would end. That I would die. Her breath penetrated my heart. Her nails dug into my back. I moved toward her slowly. She lifted her hips and grasped me in the small of my back. She wouldn't let me move, sharing my desire to stop time. I kissed her eyes. She cried. I made noises I'd never known before. She bit my lip. I felt a pleasurable pain I'd never felt before. We turned over, her on me. Only then did she take off her shirt and begin to rise and fall, slowly, without opening her eyes. I was mesmerized by the sight of her breasts, the rounded abundance and perfect nipples.

She clutched my wrists as if she were subduing me, lay down on me, and with catlike movements she clung and let go. She kissed my neck. She bit my ears. "I want you," she whispered. I couldn't understand whether she meant now or in the future. The thought that we were doing something forbidden flashed in my mind for the first time. The passion burned in me even more. I pushed her on her back and began to move inside of her forcefully. I became an animal. She moaned, also from the pain of lying on the floor. I didn't let go. I preferred that she think I was macho aggressive, not romantic thoughtful. Then she made a series of sighs that I'd never heard before in my life. Lucky, I would not have lasted one more minute. I came seconds after her. I stayed inside of her, breathing into the carpet.

I couldn't look at her. We lay there, without saying a word, for several minutes. I pulled out of her and climbed onto the bed. I put the pillow on my head. She went into the shower. What now, I asked myself. She came out wrapped in a towel, sat in front of the mirror and started brushing her hair. We stayed silent. I went into the shower. The hot, strong spray lashed my neck. I stayed in the shower for a long time, soaping my sins.

When I walked back into the room, she was already dressed. "We have work to do," she said dryly. And it hit me. What if something happens to her while I am in love? Can I behave as I am supposed to? I got dressed and we went to the bar together. We drank Campari and soda. We didn't speak. My pocket vibrated. The tracking device. Our friends were on the move.

We hurried to the car and turned on the surveillance screen.

"How are you?" I asked.

"Fine," she said. "You?"

"I don't know."

The surveillance device signaled that they were stopping. We arrived just after them. Twenty minutes outside of town, on a narrow road along the seashore. A Calypso club. Some generic name. "I'm going in," said Daria. "Take care of yourself," I said.

She wore a black wig and glasses (non-prescription, but with a tiny microphone attached to the arm), took the cellular camera (a special invention that enables daylight-quality zoom shots) and slipped in. Five minutes passed. I felt drops of sweat in my palms. Damn. I hadn't felt this way in a long time. I hadn't felt at all. What was happening to me?

"All the kids are home," she whispered. "Be careful," I replied. "I'm at the bar, they are at a table beside me." I sat in the car for about an hour. You're sweating under your armpits, I told myself. I wanted a cigarette. I quit smoking five years ago. After a few minutes, she left the club and quickly entered the car. I turned on the engine and we drove quietly down the desolate road. "A strip club," she said. "There were some very sexy girls there. Maybe you should go?"

She handed me the camera. I looked through the pictures. The two Germans could be seen in the company of two eastern-looking men showing them images of what appeared to be personal anti-aircraft missiles. Bingo. I could not help but marvel, at the information and at Daria. "Go on," she said. I looked further. Two men could be seen drinking beer while two girls sat on their laps. "Who are these guys?" I asked. "The Israelis, I guess," she said. "They were also on to them. Wait, you'll see," she added. The next picture was unbelievable. One of the girls moved from the lap of one of the Israelis and kissed one of the arms dealers on his bald spot while her friend took a picture. "Those Israelis are bastards," I hissed. "What do you care?" she said. "We got what we wanted." She was right. My ego had triggered me. "Let's go back to the hotel," she said.

We stopped at some tapas bar along the way. When we got out of the car, she looked up at the sky and took a long breath. I grabbed her from behind and kissed the back of her neck. She turned. We embraced. I knew we had fallen in love.

At the bar I ordered a whiskey. Clean. I looked at her. Panther. "Two years I've been waiting for you," she said. "Why did you wait?" I asked. "So we would be equal." I sighed. Already in the course, she had been ambitious, focused, uncompromising. "What will we give up?" I asked. "Nothing," she replied. "Nobody will know. We'll stop our activities as a team." "It's against orders," I said. "I was trained to keep secrets," she answered. "I swore to report the truth," I said, "and so did you." She said, "I have nothing to report. There's nothing. I don't remember that there was anything."

At the hotel, I gave her the honor of calling the office. "All the children feel great," she said. "I'll send pictures, you can see that we're having a great time." I liked her phrasing. On the return flight, I held myself back from holding her hand. Her smell made me dizzy, maybe because I recognized in it not only her body but also a sense of security. I'm not alone in the world.

I have no moral to share with you in that story. I just wanted to share.

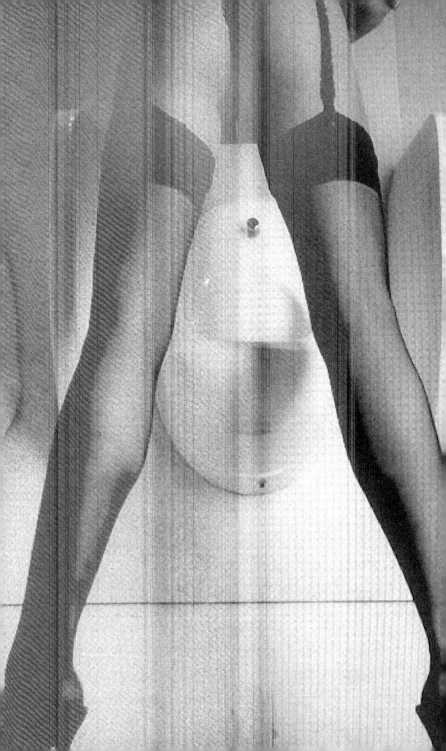

BIG MOUTH

. . . .

WORDS CAN KILL

The life of a spy is not simple. Life itself is not self-evident. The constant danger sharpens your awareness of death, but also the role you play in your life.

Life is a movie. It's a fact, not a philosophical axiom. There's something in our personality that enables us to risk our lives until death. It's not heroism, it's a genetic flaw.

Come and take – you, who do not have to take these types of risks every day – the smooth and nice part of it all. From our worldview, come and take vividness. Comfort. Coolness.

You can act the right way. You're an actor in a show. You can be a secondary actor or the lead. It's your choice. It's true that it's a real play. You can go to a hospital or to jail and say thanks if you participate to the end. But if you understand and internalize that this is all one big play – that at the end the curtain falls and all of us go home – you'll be able to free yourself, to take things lightly, to dare and take flight. Not only will she respect you more, but you will too.

In a play, the text is the anchor. "To be or not to be." Does it matter the way you read this line? Often, an agent's verbal skills determine his fate more than any other skill. You have to activate and influence strangers – with your words alone – in hotels, on the train, at airports, border stations. Courting, seducing, persuading.

There are many guidelines about the first conversation. It's not easy to make a positive impression. It's also not easy to correct a negative impression. That's why there's the concept of the opening line. Let's start by forgetting clichés like, "You look familiar…" Someone who tries to use that line with me will be met with, "Yeah, I think you sold me some shoes."

First of all, look at her. Who is she? What do her clothes say about her? What's her style? Her hair, handbag, shoes, glasses. Her body language, how she moves. Is she introverted or a social butterfly? Her body type, age, face. Did she order her drink decisively or does she have no idea what she's ordering? How does she eat, act, laugh? Maybe you don't even like her? Keep your self-confidence, but don't deteriorate into vulgarity. Gentle, polite, witty, mischievous, nonaggressive. That's the way. And the look you give before uttering that first line is like setting the ball on the white spot before the kick. Your magic touch, Maradona, begins here.

Let's take a difficult situation. Elevators. You're not alone. Ten more seconds and she's out on the street. What now? You walk out after her. "Hi. My name is Mark, sorry that I'm holding you back for a moment from the race of life. I saw you in the elevator and told myself I must meet you. This is the first time I've ever done this. Can we go for a coffee? Now, tomorrow, whenever you want. I work here, on the thirteenth floor. Business consulting."

Let's analyze: "My name is Mark, sorry that I'm holding you back." You're not some nameless guy from the street. You apologized for your interruption. You are quiet, considerate, but you follow your heart. "For a moment from the race of life." You gave her a big compliment. You see she's in a race. You understand that she's not playing a game. She has a career, she's under stress, you offer a slight respite. "I must meet you." Because you are intriguing, ignite the imagination, worth it, exciting. "Must meet" implies a missed opportunity if the meeting doesn't happen. Maybe she'll think so too. "This is the first time..." Great. You're not a serial womanizer. This time, unlike your usual custom, you gathered courage and followed your heart. "Now, tomorrow..." no pressure. You aren't going anywhere. She can go and enjoy the thought that there is something fun waiting for her. "Whenever you want." She decides. The ball is in her court. Excellent. "I work here... in business consulting." A serious guy, orderly, on his way up, also pretty busy. Surely interesting, without vanity. Beautiful.

There are more interesting situations. More extreme. Nothing to lose. You can be tougher. Go for the jackpot. In any case, if it's not intriguing and stimulating, then it doesn't really interest you, and there's no reason to pretend. You see her as an object of desire and want her to notice this between the lines. These are situations that begin with verbal wrangling, in midst of the eternal struggle between the sexes. But without fear. You are the hunter. She is the deer. She runs faster but you have the weapons. The fact is, she wants to be caught.

You: "An ordinary Nokia ringtone doesn't suit you."

She: "As long as it's not you calling, there's no problem." (Yes!)

You: "I don't call a woman whose ringtone sounds like a million other ringtones."

She: "You choose women according to their ringtone?"

You: "No. According to their personality. Their mind. Every moment, I hear a ringtone like this. How am I supposed to know if it's yours? Don't you want to feel a bit special?"

She: "I feel special. I don't need noise and ringtones to know it."

You: "Maybe you're just too lazy to change the ringtone. Maybe there's no one to change it for you. Maybe you've been using the same ringtone for a long time." (You're exaggerating a bit, the symbolism is clear.)

She: "The main thing is that I don't need to hear your little bell." (She's hurt, she fires back.)

You take a leap. You sit on her desk. "Mark McCoy. Let's grow up a bit. I guess I wanted to call you and sound special. The problem must be with me."

She: "Tanya Kahn. I just got the phone today and haven't played with the functions yet. You thought I'd get stuck with the Nokia ring? I expected more from you."

You: "Orange Champagne?"

She: "Cassis Champagne. Please."

Bingo.

ADVANCED CONVERSATIONS

This is your fourth or fifth time together. Everything is less stressful, but the road is long. There's interest, curiosity, attraction. But the criticism mechanism is starting to work, too.

How you talk, how you behave, your habits of conversation, the table layout, how much of a gentleman are you, spontaneous, cute, funny?

First of all, let her talk. Be attentive. When she talks, ask questions. Show interest. You're supposed to remember the things that she says. When you talk, don't turn into a movie track on play. Check that she's with you. Tell her true, real things, but leave room for curiosity. Don't go overboard with details. You can tell her that you once spent half a year in Mexico, there will be time later to tell her what you did there. On the other hand, you're not a headline editor at the local paper. You should expand on what happened to you while you were a barman at the Sanderson in London.

Go for two specific, enticing stories. Let her feel your moment, late at night, when Elton John left you a five hundred pound tip and you had to decide whether the money should go to the shared tip cup or straight into your pocket. Your ex-girlfriend was a cellist at the Academy of Music. You met after she came to the bar after a show at the Palace Theater. Here, don't expand. Let her fill in the blanks. "Why did it end?" It's a long story – I'll tell you one day. No rush.

When you're the talker, communicate life. Tell a story, not a grocery list. It doesn't have to be dramatic or hair-raising, but it has to show your humanity, discernment, emotion. You must understand one central issue: It doesn't matter what the actual story is. It matters how you behaved, what you thought, what mattered to you, if were you moral, whether you were generous. It really doesn't matter if it was regarding a crate of vegetables or guns, what really matters is what you did after you found a litter of cats in the crate. You see, in every story of yours, she will see herself. She'll try to predict your future together from your past. She'll tell her friend if you have a heart, if you fascinate her, frighten her, or both.

Have you asked about her parents? Sisters, brothers? Get on with it. What happens at her job? Does she like it? Who is her boss? How is he? If you haven't slept over at her place yet, when does she get up, what does she do in the morning? Does she eat something or just have a quick coffee? What's her favorite sandwich? Avocado is a good sign. Anchovies, it depends. From here, move on to her soul. What's her favorite type of music? When does she like to listen to it? Does she fall asleep quickly? Read new novels or classics? If you've gotten to the point where she admits to having a teddy bear that she's been carrying around since she was nine, you're doing good.

Movies are a great topic for conversation. If you've seen a good movie, together or separately, talk about it. The relationships, the characters. What role fascinated her, what's her opinion about the hero's mother, which moment is etched in her memory. The conversation will enable you to understand her world, her spiritual and mental depth. Same for her. Talk. At the end of the day, you're interested in someone you'll be able to talk with for the rest of your life. Going to a restaurant is just the backdrop. The heart of knowing someone, relationships in general, is conversation. It turns out that you're not a man of words. Maybe you don't have any heartwarming stories. Maybe you just woke up, brushed your teeth, studied, worked, and suddenly met her. No problem. Maybe she's also like that, and this brings joy to both of you. But I want to tell you a secret, another one.

THE DIALOGUES

This isn't a genre, but it's the base of every movie, every play, every great television series. The texts, and usually the texts between a man and a woman. The dialogues. To me, this is the ultimate creation. Take some classic film masterpieces and watch them again, the parts with the dialogues. Aside from the sheer pleasure, the elation, they can be excellent lessons in the art of conversation, speech and relationship building.

Let's take James Bond in *Casino Royale*. The novelty of this movie, compared to previous Bond movies, is the witty dialogue between 007 and his girl. Behind the scenes lies the studio's desire to turn the Bond girl from a pair of boobs into an intriguing woman with a powerful personality of her own. The dialogues between them are a pleasure for any man, experienced or rookie. Notice how the first conversation is sarcastic, clever, as if it were taking place in a wrestling arena; later comes the softening, the closeness, the mutual appreciation; and finally, the love and sharing of fate. I don't want to talk anymore about classics like *Casablanca*. Humphrey Bogart, Ingrid Bergman. "I remember…The Germans wore gray, you wore blue." Don't be disappointed if you don't reach this level. It was written by the world's best screenwriters. It's just meant to give you inspiration.

I've put together some movie titles worth watching in this context, and a few more. Here they are:

Simple People; Basic Instinct; Food, Drink, Man Woman; Thelma and Louise; Blue Velvet; Three Women; Paris, Texas;

Kill Bill; Crimes and Misdemeanors; Breathless; His Girl Friday; Taxi Driver; Manhattan; Husbands; Cries and Whispers; Pretty Woman; Bitter Moon; Chinatown; Kramer vs. Kramer; Silence of the Sheep; When Harry met Sally; Body Heat; The Usual Suspects; Casino Royale; Prizzi's Honor; The Player.

And of course, again, *Casablanca* – Bogart has inspired me more than once. The detective, the spy, the lone man in the field who always has a woman behind him, in front of him, almost never beside him. Bogart fell in love with a magnetic actress, Lauren Bacall, and played alongside her in a few movies and in the end married her. More proof that life is just one big play.

You're the star, the actor. Don't forget it. It's your key to success and pleasure. In times of distress or satisfaction, remind yourself that this is a movie. On the one hand, make the most of it. On the other hand, take things in proportion. When you have a problem, physical or mental, imagine that it's a movie, imagine what the hero would do at this moment. Do the right thing, as he would.

THERE ARE TIMES...

....

WHEN EVERYTHING GOES SMOOTHLY

We were a pair of agents, Michelle and I, on a mission in Turkey. Michelle was wearing a bikini, was wrapped in a Brazilian kanga, and I was in surfing shorts, sailing on a yacht in the Bodrum Bay. There are more difficult missions than these. We were asked to create a staged meeting (a seemingly accidental contact with a target) with Krusal, a known Turkish sailor. We tracked his activities. He had a very impressive yacht. We discovered that he went to a specific beach restaurant every afternoon. From here, the rest was easy.

Thursday, 6 p.m., Cleopatra Bay. A gray cliff slides straight into the water, seagulls float-glide, lone yachts dock nearby. The silence is deep and blue. Paradise. Krusal arrives on a small motorboat from his yacht to the restaurant. Michelle is already at the bar, pretending to be a little drunk (a basic rule in staged meetings is that you cause the target to believe that he bumped into you, not you into him).

Her phone rang. I'm on the line. "So the generator died?" she asked, giggling. "What are we going to do? How will we

find a mechanic?" she asked as she walked by him (I saw them through my binoculars from our yacht). Krusal, as befits a Turkish knight, invited her to his table, interested in the problematic generator. "My husband may not be a bad sailor, but he's got zero mechanical skills," she said, crushing my ego for the sake of the mission. "Don't worry," said Krusal, taking macho guardianship over her.

Thirty minutes later, I arrived with dirty hands (our experts prepared a burned out engine in case Krusal the professional wanted to check if our generator had really died). We sat down for a drink. I described our difficult trip in 1986 to New Zealand. We told him about the house we had recently purchased in Corfu. We invited him to a weekend at our place. "You have to come. You'll love the island. There's an airport, wonderful weather, great people." Krusal didn't blink. "On condition that you'll be my guests this evening," he answered. I agreed immediately. Michelle played the "No, thank you," but quickly agreed.

We arrived at Krusal's yacht. It was immediately clear that this was not just another yacht that couples who like to sail come to for enjoyment. There were three men on deck. Their girlfriends were presented as their wives. Whatever. A waitress in a crew uniform served us drinks. Dinner was served on the deck. We stayed until late. Krusal was a generous host, as befitting a hedonist of means. We said goodbye, exchanged emails, and went down to our small boat.

The next morning, a trained mechanic that Krusal had sent fixed the broken generator. Some burned part was replaced. What Krusal didn't know is that while we were on board his yacht the previous night, we had planted a powerful recording device and taken photos of his ship and crew. As soon as we got to our yacht, we could hear Krusal and his men talking. We passed on the communications to our people who had settled in a hotel on the beach. We weren't wrong. The information was perfect. The yacht was being used as a meeting place for arms dealers. The weapons were being transported via the Bosporus Strait to the Middle East.

I went to the embassy in Istanbul. Presented all the materials. Went back to Bodrum, straight to a fish dinner with Michelle. Krusal's yacht had disappeared from the horizon. We reported that Krusal and his men had been arrested by the Turks. The office instructed Michelle and me to stay on the yacht for a day of rest. I hid the kanga.

AND THERE ARE TIMES...

. . . .

WHEN THEY DON'T

What could possibly go wrong? Everything. Krusal could have picked up on a word that was out of place, or his technician might have recognized that the generator had burnt out long ago. A thousand and one mistakes could have buried our mission and put our lives in danger. Every day, you read about tragic cases in the newspaper, but the mind represses. It won't happen to me. But it happens. It's just a matter of statistics until it happens to you. When it comes to missions, you must take possible failures into account. In ordinary life, there's no reason to be in constant anxiety, but it's always better to be aware and to take steps to minimize risk or harm. A partial list:

- Don't lock car doors from the inside. There was an accident, you were hurt, you've lost consciousness, people will want to open the doors from the outside.
- Don't ever talk while holding your mobile phone while you're driving. Always use the hands-free mode. Don't

ever send messages while driving. Five seconds of looking at your phone is forever on the road.

- On a table or dresser next to the front door of your house, put a wallet with fifty dollars, some expired credit cards and a bunch of keys with your car manufacturer's key chain. Thieves will take the wallet (instead of going up to your bedroom), take the keys and leave. They'll try to get into the car, but of course they won't succeed and they'll probably move on to another apartment. The important thing is that your wallet, with all of your world in it, is safe and sound with you.

- If you're traveling in a strange city at night, make sure you have a couple of twenty-dollar bills in a dummy wallet, along with an old credit card. You get held up? Give the thieves that wallet. Wear a fake Rolex or a simple Swatch watch.

- Don't lock the front door to your house, or at the very least, leave the key in the lock. During a fire, there's no time to look for anything.

- Install two safes. A real one with valuables, the other one for robbers, with three hundred dollars, some worthless rings, an old watch and a couple of expired passports. Add some documents, to make it all seem real. During a violent robbery, when the burglars demand that you show them where the safe is with a pistol pointed at your temple, you'll thank me.

- Put a fire extinguisher in every room, especially in the kitchen and the children's rooms. Teach your kids how to use it. Don't be lazy, go outside with them to the yard and let them try. So that they're not afraid. I don't understand why this isn't a mandatory school activity.

- Don't leave children within a locked door or gate. Don't lock a bathroom from the inside.
- Prepare an overnight bag with everything you need for a hasty trip to the hospital. Leave it downstairs, in the coat closet.
- Don't light candles or use electric ovens before bedtime.
- Don't leave a bag or purse in your car. It will get stolen.
- Think twice before you drive in reverse. Check the area behind you.
- Until you see that your kids are buckled in, don't move the car.
- There is no situation where you should drive without a seat belt. Not even an inch.
- If you have a gun, follow all the safety rules you learned. You know what I'm talking about.
- For heavy pieces of furniture like TVs, make sure they stand steady and firm.
- If you have a pool and small children, surround the pool with a fence. Period.
- If you have to stop the car on the side of the road, don't stand in front of the car or behind it, or on the side of the road. Stand on the shoulder, only. Get all of the passengers out of the car, too.
- When you're with your wife, don't ask her to hold your mobile phone for you. You get separated by mistake – how are you going to find her?

There are many other precautions. It all depends on what you do, and the level of risk that you are in. For example, I never go into an apartment and light a cigarette without first making sure that the gas is closed in the kitchen. Every person has his own precautions. But you can add some techniques that you might never need, and perhaps one day, in some sudden moment, you actually do need. For example, set a code word with your partner that expresses distress. Let's say someone breaks into your house, ties her up and forces her to call you so that you come too. Or you escaped from your creditors to Italy, and your wife calls you and says she misses you very much and wants you to come. Your name is James. Your wife is on the phone. "James, hey honey, I'm just calling to tell you that..." 'Honey' is the code word. There's a problem. What are you going to do? Now it's your business. Call the police, come over with three thugs. The important thing is, you know there's a problem.

TAKE CARE OF YOUR BODY

....

BEFORE IT ENDS UP IN A BODY BAG

Take care of your body before it ends up in a body bag. It's as simple as that. Remember how we want her to know that you're a first-class kind of guy? A guy who knows about the street, life and women, from her head and heart all the way to her legs (forgive my bluntness)? So this chapter, which seems to be technical, is actually the base for it all. We're talking about the most fundamental habits, like shaving. There's no way to avoid it. It's a war out there.

You may think that I'm unstable, a snob, bored. But I'm none of these things. Every morning is combat and when you're outside, you're on a battlefield. Rivals are breathing down your neck, doubts are the death of you, your partners are angry, you want a promotion, the boss has his eye on you. If you're single alongside all of this, you also need to be prepared to conquer the heart of your woman. If you're a family man here, in your career, the battle is just beginning. During the day, your kids are calling you, your ex-wife is bothering you, your wife wants more attention and the other women in your life…forget it. The conclusion is clear: in the morning, you have the opportunity to stand ready at the front, both physically and mentally. There's no going back. If you leave the house like a king, there's a chance that you'll survive the day, maybe even come out on top. If you go out like a dishrag, you'll come back rung out.

Let's say you're running late and suddenly need to go to the bathroom. First thing in the morning. You've got to hold it in, run outside, ignore the call of nature, and make it to your meeting, tense and heavy. At best, the meeting was crap. At worst, you crap your pants. Is it worth it? There are some people who prefer an extra half hour of sleep over proper treatment of the body. It's a mistake, and a common one. What's the point of sleeping an extra half hour and then getting up like a slaughtered chicken and staying that way all day? I prefer to get up forty-five minutes earlier. Minutes that are spent shaving properly, sitting comfortably on the toilet if I need to, a hot shower, face cream, body lotion, getting dressed slowly, preparing a good cup of coffee (wait until the temperature drops to about 200°F, and then pour in the water, so the coffee doesn't burn) and then a relaxed exit.

It's a war outside. Mostly a mental one. Are you prepared?

FACE

It may sound obvious, but think about it for a second. Your face is the first thing a person sees when they meet you. It's your business card. Your window display. Your visual ID. In every environment. On the street, at work, in a café, on a blind date, at passport control. I recommend a cleanly shaved face. No hair. It's true, more and more men don't sanction the ritual of shaving. Thirty-five percent of young people grow a beard. Another twenty-five percent only shave once every ten days. In my opinion, the trendy stubbly look is an overreaction by the younger generation to the chores of the modern era, coupled with the high price of razors. Gillette, which controls the razor blade market, would do the world a favor by drastically lowering the prices of their blades. I predict that within a few years, the clean look will be back in fashion. In any case, if you do walk around with bristles on your face, I recommend that you look to see how your woman feels about it during intimate moments.

Check your nostrils. Every week. Don't be afraid to trim your nose hair (there's a special device for this). If you're hairy, take care of the hairs in your ears, too. Don't shave them, they'll grow back quickly and prickly. Go to a professional barber, who'll burn them for you with an alcohol-soaked stick. Don't worry, it doesn't hurt. Turkish barbers are experts. Take this opportunity to clean your ears, even before you go to the barber.

Go to a cosmetician. Let her take care of your face. She'll tell you if you have oily or dry skin. Once a month, I leave my face in the hands of Ola, a skilled beautician. Just lying on her treatment bed relaxes me. There's nothing like the hands of a trained woman to relax the day's tensions, even if you aren't a secret agent.

Apply face cream in the morning and at night. Actually, do it after every shower. For many years (too many, unfortunately)

I've been using Clinique facial moisturizer. It comes in a gray tube. Hypoallergenic, not too oily, absorbs easily, leaves the skin feeling soft. It's easy to get the cream out of the tube, the opening is just the right size, and the plastic container is light and safe for traveling. Before I go to bed, I apply nighttime cream. When I get up in the morning, I'm less wrinkled.

SHAVING

You'd be surprised by how many men don't know the secrets of shaving. Generations come and go, but a scratch on your cheek lasts. Shaving is a world unto itself, one which involves planning and execution. I'm in favor of daily shaving, in the morning. That way, you start your day clean and polished. But there are exceptions. Bristles cut best when they are a little long, after about two days of growth. Take this into consideration if you have special plans, like traveling for a day and a half, or a long night with your girlfriend, that make it worth another shave in the evening. When you go down on her, the sharp bristles under the lower lip (yours) may stab at her inner lips and clitoris, and she won't be able to concentrate on the pleasure. Already, you've started off on the wrong foot.

By the way, if you're one of those guys who doesn't like to go down on his girlfriend, we're going to have a serious conversation about it later on.

Sometimes it's best to postpone shaving in order to achieve the most satisfactory results closest to the needed time. Let's start with a common and terrible mistake: it's known that steam and hot water soften bristles, so there are men who shave after they shower. Wrong, wrong, wrong. Shaving comes before showering. Always. The act of shaving stimulates the skin, sometimes causing slight lesions or redness, not to mention accidental cuts. Hot water spraying for long minutes on your burning cheeks is good for them. A light scrub with a soft sponge, soaked in high-quality liquid soap, and rinsing with warm and then cold water, will do wonders for your skin. All those minor cuts will soften and disappear. Shaving after you shower also causes you to risk making an unforgivable mistake – showing up at work with leftover foam or soap in your ear. It's true, you can wash your face in the sink, but it's not like the shower, where the spray of the water cleans you up. The danger is too great, and no one will bother to draw your attention to it. Did any woman ever tell you that you have yellow gunk in your ears?

The razor: In the competitive world of razor-makers, there are always "inventions and innovations." Every time, one manufacturer or another claims to have made a breakthrough. Don't believe it. There can't be a breakthrough every two days. It makes more sense that every two days, there will be a new marketing gimmick. This simply means you have to be aware of the razor. Does it shave easily, elegantly, without any itching pain or bothersome tugging? How many shavings is it good for?

Method of operation: First, go in the direction of bristles. Add more shaving cream and repeat a second time, this time against the direction of the bristles, and while focusing on the more difficult areas. Only a knife that's not too worn can handle shaving against the bristles without making for pulling and scratching. Any pulling movements must be short. Rinse a lot in between. The hairs between the blades reduce a razor's effectiveness by a half. After shaving, you should be as smooth as a baby. No trace of unbeaten bristles.

Foam, cream, lotion: Here's an example of how someone who understands nothing can achieve the same result as an expert who has gone through all the steps. In the past, most shaving creams were inferior to good shaving gels. Foams were a cheap solution compared to rich gel, and the gel also required massaging to create foam. In my search for the ultimate solution, I discovered shaving foam that is better than gel by Biotherm, which gives a feeling of mousse – rich, soft, luxurious, with a high percent of humidity. It softens the bristles and feels like air.

After your (long) shower, wipe your face and let it relax, then rinse it in cold water to avoid sweating after the hot shower. Smooth and cool cheeks are an ideal place for applying facial cream.

SHOWER

After shaving, shower. Here too, show your body some respect. Take a shower twice a day, morning and evening. In the morning, for the day; in the evening, for the night. There's no way I can get into bed at the end of the day without a good shower. Your woman may come over right after work; maybe she'll come at the end of the night. I often add another shower to the menu, once after exercising and once again before going to bed. I'm not talking about having an obsession with cleanliness, it's a feeling. There's a crust, partially physical, partially imaginary, that sticks to you from the street, from the office, from wherever you are. Before you go to bed, after showering, it's better to be clean yourself from the world that sticks to you. There's nothing like crawling into new sheets with a new body. Going to sleep is like entering another world, why not come with a smile? Not to mention making love. Your body is fresh after a hot shower – it's the difference between day and night.

Regarding a shower, it's not just that the outcome is wonderful, the path is equally pleasurable. Don't go into the shower like my kids do, get wet for a second and say "I'm done." Make sure to clean all the orifices. There's nothing like water for physical and metaphysical purification. In most countries, the water is hard water and leaves the skin dry and rough. Don't use any old soap. Go for a body wash that has at least twenty-five percent moisturizing lotion. Put it on a shower sponge and enjoy yourself. Fun. If she likes to soap your back, that's crazy fun.

I like L'Occitane toiletries. They have an amazing green tea shower gel and bath oil. Both of them leave the body smooth, fragrant and moisturized. I prefer a wide shower head with a strong spray. I stay in the shower for at least fifteen minutes and prefer even twenty. The water pounding on the body has an incredible effect, one that soothes and cleanses your aura, even if you aren't aware of it. Take a look at all the nations and religions of the world, and you'll find that cleansing plays a central purification role in all of them. Don't miss out.

By the way, always finish your shower with cold water. Go slowly and gradually from hot water to cold, and try to stay in the cold water for at least sixty seconds in the morning. This is one of the most important tips I have to offer you. The cold water will keep you alert and energetic hours later and you may not believe it, but will even prolong your days on earth. Trust me.

SHIRT B

After bathing, I have a little ritual that I never miss. I call it Shirt B. You've toweled off and applied face cream and deodorant? Now put on a thin, worn T-shirt, the kind that you sleep in, some comfortable underwear, and lay quietly on your bed, on your back. Your warm body will rest and the steam rising off of it will dissolve into the cotton cloth. Be sure you tighten the shirt under your armpits so that extra deodorant is absorbed by Shirt B. Take at least ten minutes. As far as I'm concerned, read the news or just daydream. Only afterwards put on the clothes that you've chosen for the day.

WASHING YOUR HAIR

Do it every day. That's all there is to it. You know how old people have a smell? It's because they don't wash their hair. Period. Good-bye. See you later. By the way, men use twice as much shampoo as they need to. It's true for everything. You can save half of your expenses on detergents.

DEODORANT

Houston, we have a problem. What's going on?

Well, there's a serious argument that most deodorants aren't healthy. People say they are carcinogenic. This is because they contain nickel, and this can have a dangerous effect on armpit glands. There are companies that produce friendly deodorants, ones without nickel, and this is stated explicitly on the packaging. The problem is, these deodorants are less effective than those that contain nickel, and in most cases, leave you smelling worse.

A problem, as mentioned. What to do. Some women I know say that I and others like me are committing slow suicide. One thing I don't hesitate about is choosing between spray and roll-on. For me, roll-on.

CREAMS

I have drawers filled with creams. If you thought creams were just for women, you're wrong. I won't even bother explaining to you why, it's a waste of time spent on prejudice. Just believe me. I apply face cream once or twice a day, always after I shower. Face cream relieves the face and gives it flexibility. Frown wrinkles, which multiply as you age, won't disappear, but at least they'll soften. It's important to apply cream around the eyes, to the forehead, to the neck.

I use body lotion on my neck and the nape of my neck. If I run out of the right cream, I use face creams that I don't really like anymore. I find them a new vocation, spreading them on my elbows, knees, heels and the back of my neck. It's an area prone to trouble, gets rough, dry, wrinkled. Apply a rich cream lightly to the skin. An old cream that has really passed its prime I use on my boots. What's wrong with that?

I don't know if you watched "Sex and the City", a must-see for every man, but in one episode Samantha was shocked to discover the dwindling backside of her elderly partner. Biology is a cruel thing, and this is another reason to apply body lotion to the buttocks. I already told you that women are crazy about our asses, didn't I?

One more trick. I put body lotion on my feet. Just like that, when I go out. And when I get home from work, I have delicate feet like a chicken, soft, like after being boiled in fine wine. Women want us rough, but not our feet. So let's leave rough feet to the people running barefoot in the desert. I've been there. It's nothing great.

Many men have a fetish for the female foot. Your own feet should be clean and well-groomed, exactly like the fingers on your hands. You need a mani-pedi once every two months, at least. Again, if you think it's not manly, think again. Don't be a sucker for norms. Cut your fingernails religiously. Women want a man in bed, not an eagle. Look at your nails. Do you see any yellow-brown decorations? It appears mainly on the big toe and if you see it, you should know: it's fungus. You won't die from it, but it's ugly. You can buy a liquid or cream that gets rid of it at any pharmacy. It takes a long time for it to go away, and you have to apply the cream regularly for about a month. If the problem is more widespread, go to a dermatologist. No arguing.

Listen closely. When a man shows up to meet a woman wearing flip-flops, he's already off to a bad start. If he's also got long toenails that are already starting to curve upwards, it's the first thing that she's going to notice. The first mark against you, to be exact. A warning sign. If you have long toenails *and* you're a cheapskate, there is no way she's going to let you sleep with her, and not with her dog, either. If she does, get rid of her. She's desperate.

HAIRSTYLE

Hair can dazzle, but only if the length suits you. We already talked about washing your hair every day. The same principle applies to getting a haircut. Find a barber that understands hairstyling. Make sure you get your haircut on time. Not when the situation is serious, but the day before you look your best. You can't go around morning and night with a bad hairstyle. It's not cool. Moreover, make sure that you double-check the top of your head. At some point you'll see signs of balding, well before the stage when you have a plate in the center. Don't wait for this stage.

Immediately in the early stages of baldness, get a short haircut. As the baldness progresses, go for a buzz cut. In more advanced stages, start cutting your hair with a shaver, almost shaving, and at the end, shave your head entirely. It's a clever trick. People will get used to seeing your short hair, and they won't be shocked by the change. A shaved head suits many men, and is considered sexy by many women.

AFTERSHAVE AND COLOGNE

I won't tell you which one to use. It's an individual thing. So what will I say? Learn, develop an understanding. Go to pharmacies, Duty-Free shops, try them. Spray a tester on your wrist. Wait a minute and then smell. Take your woman with you, ask her what she likes. Try two different scents, each in a different place. Test them. There are sweet ones and there are woody ones.

Light, sour, lemony, fresh ones – these are for the summer. Heavy, sweet, powerful, dramatic ones – these are for winter.

The white, naughty ones – these are for day. Serious, dignified ones – for night.

I believe that you need one fragrance that is your own. A scent identified with you. "That's Mark's smell," she should say, not "That's Calvin Klein's fragrance." That's why you must choose one cologne and stick with it. Don't choose a fashionable scent, but one that will last for a long time. Something classic. Choose one for summer, for every day, and one for winter, for night. Take note. There's aftershave and there's cologne. What's the difference? Cologne is more concentrated. A spritz or two in the right places. Splash aftershave in the morning; cologne at night.

Where to spray? The sides of the neck, behind the ears, the pulse points on the wrists, the sides of the groin. Sometimes I spray lightly on my underwear, just for the sake of it. Wherever you spray, don't overdo it. You don't need to smell like you work in a perfume factory. It must be subtle and intriguing, lightly felt and disappearing. Mysterious. If you're going to make love or make out, use less.

Don't buy a lot at one time. After a year, fragrances lose their smell. Don't let the cologne or aftershave interfere with the smell of your deodorant. Spritz a bit of cologne in the car, just a drop. And despite the desire to stay with the same fragrance forever, don't forget to stay on top of things and change. Maybe the scent that your ex liked so much isn't to the liking of your current woman.

THE BATHROOM

You must have already figured out that I see the bathroom as the operations room. If you're the weapon, the bathroom is the armory. Enjoy it. Arrange the creams, aftershave, razors, foam, deodorant, toothbrush, electric shaver, clippers, tweezers, and more. Like the most luxurious suite that you ever saw in a movie. Everything is arranged in my drawers like complete sets of soldiers. I don't "run out" of anything. It's terribly silly to run out and buy things when you have to. It's much more pleasant to buy in advance. I usually do this when I travel. As though the time you wait for your flight was intended for a large, concentrated purchase. I already know exactly what I'm looking for, and usually buy seven or eight of everything.

In addition to all of the toiletry and grooming products that I use every day, I also prepare a bag with an extra set of toiletries. Why repack every time? In fact, I have four complete sets. One in the bathroom, one in the suitcase I take when I travel, one at the gym and one in my car.

It's all about giving yourself some respect. You stand in the bathroom at least twice a day, you look in the mirror, you look around you. A pleasant woman and pleasant tools expand a man's mind. Start in the bathroom. There's no reason for you to feel like a king only in a luxury spa. There's nothing like starting the day like a king. By the way, they used to say, "I'm going to the room where the king also goes alone." If you don't buy the best toilet paper in the store, you have a lot to learn.

Imagine George Clooney's bathroom. Beautiful bottles arranged on the countertop. A sense of luxury and richness that can be smelled from every corner. Don't you deserve this too? One of the hallmarks of a stupid young bachelor is a cracked sink, a toothbrush with worn bristles, a squeezed tube of toothpaste, dried foam on the shaving cream. Learn something important. You may not be able to buy a Ferrari, but a bathroom like George Clooney's you can prepare in a day. Amal will follow.

DAWN OF A NEW DAY

························

BREAKFAST IS EATEN THE MORNING, THE QUESTION IS, WHEN IN THE MORNING

There was a time when I went to London every few weeks. Meetings and appointments that required formal wear. We would put on the costume (a suit and tie) and go down to the impossible-to-refuse breakfast. The amazing abundance, ever more tempting options – eggs, breads, jams, quiches, vegetables, fried sausages, bacon, and all the other wonders of a seventy-euro breakfast.

My advice? Don't start this way. One or two espressos, some sparkling mineral water and you're in control. Because you're light. Muhammad Ali's secret wasn't in his terrifying fists, it was in his ease of movement. Float like a butterfly. Remember: Movement is the key. In the office, in bed. If you're heavy – you're dead. Why do single men go out so much? Because they don't eat at home. If they eat, they don't go out. When I make a date with my girlfriend for a drink, I warn her not to eat before we go, and follow this rule tenfold myself. A person who is full is not interesting. His libido is busy with his digestion system rather than his loins. Busy with his own ass instead of hers.

In any case, on one of those maddened mornings at the Langham Hilton, the waiter spilled a soft-boiled egg on me. I wore a white linen shirt and beautiful blue tie, and the egg yolk streamed down my tie, in front of my astonished eyes, creating a permanent stain. That morning was particularly important, a morning of enlightenment. On that day, I deciphered the code of men who are not enslaved to conventional behavior, but who make their own rules.

It goes like this. You're overseas? At a hotel? Breakfast? Meeting? Everything is fine. Get out of bed and brush your teeth quickly. No more than that. Throw on a sweat suit or some tennis clothes and go downstairs to breakfast. Just the way you are. Don't let those snakes in suits cloud your thoughts. They're slaves. Trapped by the system. Drink some coffee, have a bite to eat, read the newspaper. Relax. Have a poached egg (not fried), have some fresh salmon. Don't worry about crumbs. For all I care, get a deep yellow stain on your shirt. Pour another cup of coffee, have a long yawn. Finished?

Now that you are light, relaxed and at ease, when everything is in just the right proportion, go back to your room and begin treating your body properly, as described in the previous chapter. The entire ceremony. Masturbate, flatulate, brush, shave, shower. Rinse off the night with the early morning. Spread moisturizer on your face, aftershave, put on your best clothes and go downstairs, dressed like a prince for your important meetings.

Do me one small favor: When you leave the hotel, take a

look at the mummified men who have to eat as though they are frozen, fearful that at any moment, their food will end up on their slacks instead of in their stomachs. And by the way, if we're already talking about stomachs, if you managed to take a dump before you showered and dressed, you scored. Hotel toilets are filled with fat men holding the tips of their ties between their teeth as they try the impossible – to take a dump while wearing a suit and not get it creased. Ridiculous.

MAN'S BEST FRIEND

·····························

WHEN YOU HAVE TO SHOOT, SHOOT

In my opinion, you should have a gun. I also think you should know how to use it. In my opinion, a man who doesn't know how to shoot is like a man that doesn't know how to drive. You don't even need to hit live targets, just knowledge, practice and carrying weapons expands your horizons. The secrets of drawing and shooting your weapon can certainly save your ass, but more than that, they imbue you with peace, confidence and strength, much like judo and other forms of martial art.

Professional gun shooting is based on having a cool disposition, restraint and concentration, qualities that are an asset to every man. A three-month operational shooting course will bring you to a fairly high level of expertise. It's true that your chances when faced with a skilled professional will still be very low, but the goal is to get you to react to a random attack, when all that's required of you is reasonable self-defense. In shooting, there are two different elements, two skills that can be applied to any area of life:

- The ability to shoot accurately based on experience and inner peace.
- Quick movement, agility, and spatial orientation, all of which are the fruits of concentration and focus.

The base of shooting is breathing. Yes, breathing. The very awareness required for something as obvious as breathing is an incredible discovery that will bring you to heights you never knew before. I practiced with a gun for eight months, six days a week. One of the stages is called "The Room." That simple. The room. You're in a huge, dark room. Absolute darkness, blacker than black. There are all kinds of cardboard boxes on the floor and sounds from the street: a passing train, thunder, industrial plant noises. Suddenly, unexpectedly, you hear a man's voice. Two seconds. Four words. You have to pull out your gun and shoot. Four bullets in two clusters. You must hit him in the torso. It's hard. After dozens of days of training, most trainees have a fifty percent success rate.

The entire scene takes about six minutes, but when you leave the room, you're sweating and exhausted as though you've been running for an hour. Do you know what you learn in this lesson? To breathe. Don't hold your breath. Fear is paralyzing. Don't be afraid. It doesn't help. That's the lesson. That's the life lesson I want to teach you. You can do it. Just breathe and believe. Believe that you have power, the charisma. That you can convince people. You must believe that you're capable. After that, she'll believe in you. After that, everyone will.

EVERYTHING IS POSSIBLE

....

HOW SELF-CONFIDENCE & RESOURCEFULNESS WILL HELP YOU GO FAR

Why does this matter? All you have is yourself. Your face, your mouth. Go into a convenience store. You don't have a penny. Convince the clerk to give you a free pack of cigarettes. Tell him you'll bring the money tomorrow. Can you do it? A thousand smart alecs have done the same thing before you. Start thinking. Try it yourself. Breathe. A convenience store is just one example. There are dozens of others. Here's a random list.

PARKING

A man who looks for a parking spot while assuming he won't find one is a loser. A winner is someone who always thinks there's a parking spot with his name on it. At big events – parties, plays, weddings, or anywhere else where there are more invitees than parking spots – don't start looking for parking at the far end of the lot. Go straight to the first few rows. It's really quite simple: There will always be someone who left early. Or someone who had to leave suddenly. Or maybe just an emp-

ty spot that others skipped over. In ninety percent of cases, I find a spot. If there are valet attendants directing cars, ignore them. Go straight to the entrance. Everything will be fine, you just have to have faith. As for the lady at your side, don't say a word. Drive in confidence. If it turns out that there isn't any parking, simply let her out beside the door. "I brought you straight to the entrance," tell her. "I'll go find parking now." You come out on top this way too. If they don't let you drive past the entrance, explain that you're bringing someone to the wedding, let her out of the car and go.

Think like a winner. Be resourceful. There's always some guy who is in charge of something. Take the band's driver, for example. Give him your car keys, a ten dollar tip, and ask him to take care of things. If a spot frees up, tell him to park the car and leave the keys with the guy at the front door, the concierge, the guard, his sister. Take the initiative, it's no big deal. You can always find the bride and groom's car and block it. They're not going to leave before you, right? Start thinking big. It's always cheaper to buy big.

Let's say the parking lot really is full. There's always those guys in the car wash. Leave them the car; it probably needs a good cleaning, anyway. How much could it possibly cost? At plays, concerts, shows, park the car where it says "Reserved," or be even more assertive: put a sign on your windshield that says "Production Team" and go into the show. Where'd you get the sign? You have one ready in your car. Any graphic studio can prepare one.

Another thing. If you go to a huge event – a rock show at a stadium or a Lakers playoff game – take a helium balloon with you and tie it with a string to your side mirror. When you leave the game, drunk with victory, you'll find your car in a second. She'll admire you. Also, keep a bottle of water in the car, along with some candy and gum. After all, you're going to want some. Why stand in line with all the losers after the game?

GOING OUT

You'll probably want to get something to eat or drink something afterwards, and every place will be packed with wise guys like you. Reserve a table at three different places in the area. A well-known steakhouse, a high-end Italian restaurant, a trendy bar. Ask her what mood she's in. Whatever she says, you're prepared. Be a man – let the other two places know you're not coming. No harm done.

As a rule, try to be a regular at the good restaurants. They'll get to know you and things will be easier for you. Have a word with the people in charge of reservations. Remember their names. Now, you call and try to reserve a table. Let's talk about the situation that there is room. If you're a couple, ask for a table for three. If you're a foursome, say you're five. You'll get a better and bigger table. What's the benefit? You'll have an extra chair for your jackets, handbags, etc. What if her girlfriend suddenly wants to join you. You're a king – you've anticipated everything.

Now, let's say you call to reserve a table and there's no room. In my world, there's no such thing. A negative answer is the beginning of a dialogue. Be indifferent, charming, clever. Share the secret of your troubles with the host. Tell her that this is an important blind date, mention that you're excited and that it's important to you. She'll soften. Make her feel compelled to help you. Turn her into your partner in crime. After all, if she had to find a place for her father, she'd succeed, wouldn't she?

Tell her that an investor from overseas is coming for just one night and that this is the most suitable restaurant for hosting him. Be creative. Use your head. Share your brilliance with the world. Restaurant hosts usually work part-time. Show interest in her. Ask what she's studying. Imagine she's studying psychology, and your uncle is one of the city's most respected psychologists. See, she needs you. From here, the path to a reservation is short.

Ask about smoking, non-smoking tables. On the patio, at the bar. Try a different time. Be flexible. The most important thing is that the two of you are partners in trying to find a table. You're in this together. Once you're inside, everything is possible. Someone will cancel at the last minute, you'll move to sit where you want to. Don't forget to say thank you. Both with personal attention and with a tip. Cheapskates always lose.

THE MOVIES

Going to a movie is the most worthwhile date around, the best return on your investment. Why do I say this? From today onwards, you're not two people – you are four. This is one of the most important tips I have to give you, and one of the easiest ones to implement. From now on, you don't buy a pair of tickets for the movies, you buy four of them.

You go into the theater with her, row ten in the middle. If you bought four tickets, the seat to the right will be empty as well as the seat on the left. No one will be breathing on her, no one will make her nervous. There's room for your jackets, you don't have to fight with anyone over the armrests. Don't tell her. You're already showing flair. Let her marvel at your good luck, how there were exactly two empty seats right next to you. The next time, she'll really be impressed. The third time, she's supposed to understand that you had a hand in it. Smooth. The first time, she'll be impressed by the idea; the next time, she'll be impressed because you didn't tell her. Sure, you invested a couple bucks more in every date, but look what you got in return. No thug will end up sitting beside her, you can switch seats if someone is blocking her view. Classy.

If you bought bad seats for the theater, note the mistake. It shouldn't happen. The people sitting near the exits are financing the show for people in the good seats. It is as if your seat on a plane is the baggage compartment. I don't buy bad seats for the theater, period. Nevertheless, if you still managed to find yourself in a terrible spot at the theater, relax. Nothing is final until you finalize it. Go to the front of the theater, where the best seats are. Leave your date in the original seats. She just needs to be on the alert for your text message. Now, look for empty seats. Go for the jackpot. Look in rows four to eight. Found a space? Wait until one minute before the show starts. Anyone who hasn't arrived until then won't show up at all. If they do, they'll be taken to the gallery. I already told you that the gallery is for losers. You need to understand – there's a ninety percent chance that somebody won't show up. An accident, sudden illness, fight, mistake, there's no shortage of reasons. Usually, those are the most expensive seats, too. Those people don't really care if they paid but don't show up. Now, sit nonchalantly in your royal seat. Send a message to your date telling her the row and seat. It's that simple.

WIMBLEDON

In one of the final exams, we were a team of four. They dropped us off at Wimbledon, an hour before the final match. The mission: To get in without tickets and find a seat in the Royal Box. Right next to the queen. You read it right – no tickets at all.

We acted wisely. Two of us wore security guard outfits (cheap suits) and earpieces (from mobile phones). Your faithful servant wore a suit and sunglasses, and they shielded me while shouting, "Don't take pictures, please," at our fourth friend, who was walking backwards in front of us wearing a photographer's jacket, two cameras around his neck, and a press badge. The funny thing is that other photographers gathered and took pictures of me, even though they had no idea at all who they were chasing for a photo. We found a vacant seat in the Royal Box. A lovely girl opened the rope for us. "Good afternoon, Mr. ....", "Good afternoon, honey." We sat. It was nice.

During the third set, the chairman of Mercedes, his wife, their daughter and some other guest were amazed to find their seats in the prestigious box occupied. Don't worry. It ended with an invitation to a private Caribbean vacation the next morning. Who said an agent's life is difficult?

CHEERS!

. . . .

NOW, TIME FOR SOME WINE...

You know those people who say, "I don't drink at work"? To me, that's like saying, "I don't live at work." I love wine. There are some people whose sense of smell and taste don't connect with wine. Too bad for them. Before you give up, make sure you've given it your best shot. What do I mean? You need to drink good wines, at the right moment, with the right food. Find a friend who likes wine and understands it a bit. Ask him to join you in your efforts. A perfect man needs to understand wine at least enough so that he can talk about it with his woman. Wine is a perfect accompaniment to a relationship. To help you with your little problem, here's a guide that will make you an expert in ten minutes.

A note before starting: If you're the kind of person who takes a bite of food, swallows and then washes it down with wine, you're making a mistake. An epic fail. Wine, like a kiss, is slow and thorough. First, sip calmly, let the wine coat the inside of your mouth and tongue. Then, let the food settle slowly on the layer of wine. Now, you can enjoy both the taste of the food and of the wine. Bon appétit.

***

Wine is like a living being. It may be young or old, strong or interesting, casual or exciting, and so on. Even more beautiful is that there is a striking connection – to the point of an amazing match – between wine and the country it comes from. In order to describe wine in the most enlightening way possible, just think about the characteristics of the place from where it came.

FRENCH WINES

Respect. Legacy. This can't be taken from them. They live a little bit on past glory. They take themselves seriously, are filled with power, have dominant smells, sometimes stink, come from deep dark cellars with cold stone walls, European quality that doesn't suck up nor try to impress. French wines are proud and aggressive. There are some rare wines and some terrible failures. Either way, French wine is always stubborn, always goes its own way – it has a rich and glorious history, but refuses to recognize the modern world.

ITALIAN WINES

Song, opera, joy, style. Italian wines have huge success alongside national failures, they are wines that forgive themselves and the people who drink them, wines that are sexy and varied – like a quick blow job at lunchtime and a long passion-filled night. Full-bodied wines are like a plump opera singer; light-bodied wines are like a lean man in a Vespa.

Italian wines are sure of themselves but not condescending, wines that taste good but don't make an effort to be incredible. At the same time, they are unstable and sporadic. One day a Ferrari, the next day a Fiat.

AMERICAN WINES

Relatively new in the world, quite comfortable, not too blunt, pleasant, confident, able to live comfortably with themselves without being moved by the old world. American wine is like a Jeep Cherokee: leather seats, pampers when you're off-road, looks big and powerful, but has a weak engine compared to the body. Disciplined and orderly wine that is also stable. Almost no disappointments. There are excellent American wines, but major successes are rare.

GERMAN WINES

Sorry about the cliché, but these are the most precise wines in the world, with clear flavors and scents. The Germans have mostly white wines, very cold. German wines are arrogant, safe and distant. They go best with a precise meal at a specific time. Before choosing a German wine, there is always a slight hesitation, but in the end, the choice is successful. One might say that German wines aren't exactly old world, but they aren't new world, either. They are in a world of their own, somewhat oblivious to what is happening around them. Denial, anyone?

ISRAELI WINES

Not bad wines at all, even if they do rely too often on one-off successes. Israel's history of wine dates back to biblical times, but it is only in the last decade that a real wine culture began developing. Some of the improvisations aren't half-bad, but when it comes to being consistent, they tend to get lost. Israeli wines are presumptuous, much like Israelis themselves, and suffer from a lack of patience – everything must be quick and now. Nevertheless, today there are several serious wineries in Israel that succeed in producing very good wines year after year, wines with grades ranging from ninety to ninety-six.

NEW ZEALAND AND AUSTRALIAN WINES

Surprising New World wines. Every encounter with an Australian wine is a surprise, primarily because you don't know what to expect. New Zealand surprises with some stunning white wines, with a combination of earthy flavors and a spirit that's not quite clear. The wine makes you want to know more. They are considered remote but are very cordial in the first drink, encouraging. Sometimes they have a baseness and earthiness to them, but then suddenly you discover a new and fascinating taste. You can certainly talk about something marginal that's about to take center stage. Australian and New Zealand wines are slowly making their way toward world recognition, without being pushed and with considerable self-confidence. They aren't in a hurry. As if they are saying, you'll discover us, it's just a matter of time.

THE DIFFERENCE BETWEEN WHITE AND RED WINES

Just like storks don't really bring children to the world, red wines aren't squeezed from red grapes and white wines aren't born from green ones. After the harvest, grapes are crushed and transferred to a winepress, and from there to fermentation tanks. It's here that the color is determined – white wines ferment without grape peels, red wines ferment with them. In white wines, there is a process of refining, filtering and bottling. In red wines, the process is a bit more involved. I'll save you the trouble. The main thing is that red wines are given longer to age in the barrel.

TEMPERATURE

A dramatic issue. Wine that isn't served at the right temperature loses its flavor and charm. White wines are served at fifty to sixty degrees Fahrenheit (refrigerate until just before serving). Light red wines: Sixty degrees. Heavy red wines: Seventy degrees (remove from the refrigerator about one and a half hours before serving).

What's light and what's heavy? I'll teach you the tricks. Think about thick, rich chocolate milk versus thin, light chocolate milk. It's not exactly the same thing, but it's a way to remember. Here are a few more key concepts.

TANNIN

Acid found in the grape's skin. Slightly bitter. Tannin protects the wine for a long period of time.

ASTRINGENCY

A stiff, dry sensation in the mouth caused by high tannin. Reminiscent of a bite of unripe fruit. Click your tongue and say, "This wine is high in tannins. It will last for a good long time," and you'll sound like a winner.

AROMA

A wine's smell. Its source is the grape and the processes it's been through. Wine connoisseurs like to talk about a wine's smell and taste using their own terms. Don't worry, I'll teach you these too.

BODY

The body. This refers to whether the wine has a full and strong presence or if it is weak and thin. Think back to the chocolate milk. In wine, body is very important. In full-bodied wines, the flavor lasts after swallowing. It leaves its mark. If drinking it was like drinking light juice, say: "It wasn't bad, but if you ask me, it lacks body." If the sip was enjoyable and filled with strength, you can say: "Guys, we've got a wine with serious body here."

BOUQUET

The bouquet, in contrast to the aroma, is the smell that sticks to the wine as a result of the aging and bottling process. Aroma is related to the type of grape and the fermentation process. Simply put, bouquet is the smell obtained from the aroma (the smell of fresh grapes) and from the smells generated after a long stay in the barrel.

ACIDITY

A sour taste that comes after the wine comes in contact with the air (oxidation). Contact with the air is necessary for refining the taste of the wine, which essentially lay sealed and closed for years.

AFTERTASTE

The taste of the wine lingers in the mouth even after swallowing. This taste is called the aftertaste.

DRY, SEMI-DRY

This refers to the wine's sweetness. A little sugar – dry. More sugar – semi-dry.

TYPES OF WINES: WHITES

Sauvignon Blanc – One of the most popular varieties. A very pleasant wine, usually dry and refreshing.

Chardonnay – Very popular and successful, maybe the most popular in the world. One of the only white wines that is aged in wooden barrels. A floral wine (Don't be alarmed. It just means that the wine is fragrant like flowers or fruit).

Riesling – Rich and fragrant wine. Comes mostly from Germany and France. There are some excellent varieties.

TYPES OF WINES: REDS

Cabernet Sauvignon – The king. Originally from France, Bordeaux I think. A wine that can age for many years. Usually full of body and deep-flavored.

Merlot – The Queen. A round, softer wine. Very famous.

Pinot Noir – Interesting, French. Not very stable, due to its sensitivity.

Petite Sirah – Dominant. I never got along with this one.

TYPES OF WINES: ROSÉS

Very cute. A production process between white and red, the grape juice gets a bit of color from the peels and then they are removed. Rosé wines are sometimes an excellent compromise when you don't know whether you should choose white or red. These wines are served chilled, primarily during the day, and are suitable for fish, seafood, light cheese, pasta in cream sauce, and more.

TERMS FOR TASTE AND SMELL

A conversation between two wine connoisseurs can sound arrogant and absurd, but to be fair, it's very difficult to talk about a wine's smell and flavor without being dragged into fancy words and flowing images. That's why such words have associations that preserve the romance of drinking. Let's say you wanted to describe the yellow of the full moon rising. Instead of being satisfied with "yellow-like..." or "desert-like...," you could say, in excitement, something nostalgic like, "the yolk of the moon as it rises." Kapish? That's how wine people tend to use words like earth, light, smoke, tobacco, chocolate, grass, lemon, butter, tree, cellar, etc. Take advantage of this approach. All you need to do in order to describe wine is to sniff the glass and understand the association it makes. You can say in wonder, "Earth after the rain."

USER'S MANUAL

When you (or the wine waiter) pour the wine, make sure that the glass becomes only partially full. Swirl the cup on the table and let the wine "open up," that is, come into contact with the air. The scent will be released, you'll be able to dip your nose into the glass and lightly smell the aroma. That way, you'll be able to understand and talk about the smell. Wine, like you, really needs to breathe. Especially after it has been held captive in a barrel or bottle and is suddenly set free. The only thing it wants is air. Easy, no?

The beauty of wine is that after all of the descriptions, it speaks for itself, opens up with joy and gives of itself easily. So forget the nonsense, open a good bottle, at the right moment (before the food), at the right temperature, in a big glass, pour a bit, wait a moment, smell, taste, and say to her: "This wine is really perfect for us – filled with passion, wild, connected to the earth, to the cherry, to us, just we we are." Cheers!

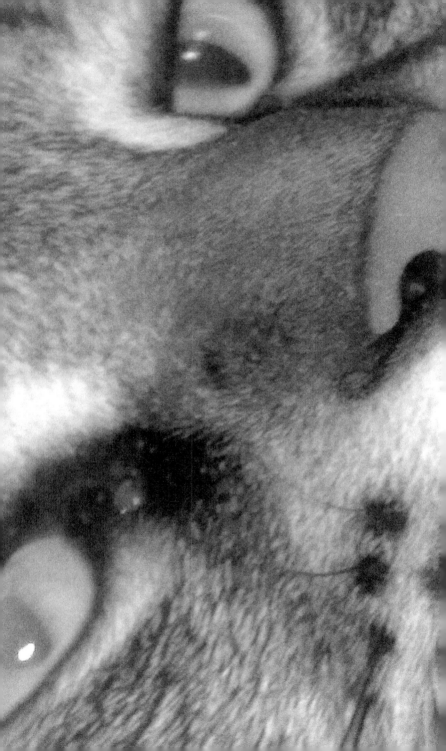

A WELL- OILED MACHINE

....

THE IMPORTANCE OF EXERCISE, NOT TO MENTION MASSAGE, CANNOT BE OVERSTATED

Where there is a hit out on someone, they're aware of the danger hovering over them. They change habits, addresses and plans from one moment to the next, surrounded by guards and technological gadgets that make it difficult to locate them. As soon as a purple file is opened (indicating that a target that needs to be removed), the smallest details about that person are collected. Planning must be based on zero mistakes. A mistake is something that causes the target to become even more careful and evasive.

A few years ago, we encountered a particularly hard nut to crack. This guy had nine lives, eyes at the back of his head, and the luck of a serial lottery winner. He changed cars like other people change socks, would buy tickets to five different destinations and at the last moment, board a sixth flight. Careful study of the information revealed that in the area of his home, his offices and his restaurants, the mission was complicated, even impossible. And then, I was sent to the city where he lived.

We got our break. The man worked out with a personal trainer at a luxury gym, in a private room that was rented out by the hour to VIPs. I signed up for the gym. I discovered that VIPs have personal lockers. The lockers were in a closed room. His locker was easy to spot. It was the only one with two locks. The lockers were installed against a wall, and behind the wall was a spinning studio.

Friday night, late, we broke into the gym. We didn't break into the locker room, we broke into the spinning room, drilled a hole in the wall, and sawed open the back of his locker. In our first attempt, we reached the locker above his. Turns out that the height of the floors in the rooms was not equal. We recalculated and succeeded in our second attempt. In the locker, we found what we were looking for: protein powder that dissolves in water, for consumption after exercise. We added to the protein powder some highly advanced poison that is lethal once it comes into contact with water. To be on the safe side, we also put a bit of the powder in the measuring spoon. We closed the back of the locker so that the cut wouldn't be visible from the inside. We repaired the hole in the spinning room wall and hung a poster of a cyclist over the repair. Mission accomplished. We slipped out.

Three days later, after a strenuous workout, our target sat down at the gym bar, prepared for himself a heaping dose of protein shake, drank it from a glass, and went to take a shower. He died clean. The press talked about someone dying after a particularly intensive workout. It would be interesting to know how many trainers dropped their pace a notch after that episode. A clean takedown, without any scent or signs, just like it should be, with a moral on the side: after a workout, it's best to drink just water.

***

You need to work out, period. To be fit. There's no way you can't run for at least three kilometers. Running can be a matter of life and death. You may find yourself in a situation where you run after someone or away from them, in both cases, you need to run. You may have to run up twenty flights of stairs. In short, your heart needs to withstand any burden that it meets.

Fitness isn't just important for cardiovascular endurance. You also need to exercise in order to develop muscle strength and flexibility. Don't underestimate flexibility. I highly recommend taking yoga classes, Feldenkrais, body cognition classes, or any other type of exercise that contributes to muscle flexibility. I recommend investing two to three years in some type of martial art – judo karate, aikido, boxing. This will introduce you to specialized areas. Senses, coordination, flexibility, reaction speed and more than anything else, exceptional confidence.

The bulk of what you learn is applied long before the first blow. It is the quiet, the concentration and the understanding of the body that helps you act like a well-oiled machine. The thought, the release of tension, the relaxation of muscles, the breathing. When a person is afraid, he stops breathing at the exact moment when he needs a lot of oxygen. Have you ever seen a dancer? How much air does he need?

It's best if you have a sporty hobby. Some popular sports, like tennis, look great in photos, but they aren't great for the body. Why? Because they aren't symmetrical and they activate one side of the body more powerfully than the other. Look carefully at the body of a serious tennis player. You'll notice the difference between their serving hand and the other one. That's the obvious difference, but it signals a deeper problem – imbalance between the two sides of the body. Every action of the back and twisting around the spine occurs around a single axis only. The result is that one side is long and stretched while the other side is short and shriveled. Even golf – a seemingly adult sport – leads to back pain, imbalance, problematic posture, and similar. Next.

THE GYM

Most people who work out at gyms are busy lifting weights. The result is inflation of the muscle. It's an illusion. It takes a year to get results, and a month to lose them. If training is done with close guidance from a qualified trainer, you can work correctly and achieve the desired result. The correct method is based on working with light weights and many repetitions. At the end of every exercise, you need to stretch thoroughly in order to lengthen the muscle and avoid contractions. Very few people are careful about this. It requires patience, perseverance, discipline and understanding.

AEROBIC ACTIVITY

Aerobic activity improves cardiorespiratory fitness and burns calories. The most common activities are running, walking and cycling. You can combine all of them. Train for at least forty-five minutes every time. You must reach at least five kilometers at every work out, ideally seven or eight. You should walk or run at least two or three times a week, every other day. Run on a synthetic track or sand to protect your joints. For the same reason, you need shoes that are meant for running. Your running style should be light, flexible, without heavy pounding, and you shouldn't start running without warming up and stretching first. After you run, rest until your heartbeats slows and then do some basic stretching for about ten minutes. It's best to go into a sauna or steam room to relax the body.

You must do aerobic exercise like running. If someone ever chases after you, it's unpleasant to be caught after a hundred yards. You'll never know when you'll have to climb a rope, run up the stairs or chase down a pickpocket. Not to mention sex. If, after intense sexual activity, you're gasping for air, don't be surprised if she dumps you for a diver.

There's another reason. Humanity suffers from depression much more today than in the past. Beyond the usual reasons – financial insecurity and anxiety – there's a sense of loneliness today that didn't exist in the past. Society has become withdrawn, the human community has moved to the internet, a world without faces and contact. Over and over again, studies show that there is nothing like physical fitness for dealing with depression, sometimes enabling total release from it. Swimming, walking, running, and basically any aerobic exercise that releases endorphins makes us feel good about ourselves. Thirty minutes of exercise every day may be more effective than a pill.

FLEXIBILITY

Maintaining flexibility is the most important activity. If you thought yoga, Feldenkrais and the like are for women and old people, think again. How do you identify old age? By the rigid body, the inflexibility, the hunched back. Don't grow old prematurely. You must preserve long muscles and flexible joints. The more you work on flexibility today, the more your body will thank you tomorrow.

There are many activities for developing flexibility. The most basic is daily stretching. It's something that's very measurable and can be tracked. Stand upright with your legs stretched and try to reach the floor with your fingers. Don't fake it. Check and start working. My trainer is sixty years old and can reach the floor with his wrists. A flexible and elastic body means less pressure on the vertebrae and this means fewer back problems, something that most men suffer from.

GYRO

The Rolls Royce of flexibility is called Gyrotonic, also known simply as Gyro, which is enhanced Pilates. If there is no Gyro at your Pilates studio, find another studio. Gyro training requires special certification. Find out where the best institute is near you and go there. Practice with a personal trainer, at least twice a week. To make things easier on your wallet, you can join a group class once a week. In this world, anyone with brains and money does Gyro. Madonna does it every day. No joke. Gyro will develop your body and bring you to new fronts. The real gift, a strong and flexible body, you'll understand over the years. Anyone who trains in Gyro will look younger than his age forever. Any time they wanted to send me to some destination, I asked for only two things: a gym with a running track and a personal Gyro instructor. London, New York, Amsterdam, Lisbon, Paris, Johannesburg, Rome, Tel Aviv. I never give it up. Especially not in Tel Aviv. At the Hilton Hotel in Tel Aviv I would run on the beach, look at the gorgeous Israeli women, and go to the Gyro studio across the street from the hotel with one of the best instructors in the world. If I remember correctly, her name was Ruth or Reut. Reut, during the American invasion of Iraq, I disappeared on you. I apologize.

MASSAGE

Here's an activity that's fun and important. Who says you have to suffer to enjoy? I recommend a one-hour massage every week. It's not cheap, but it pays off in the long run. It must be a professional massage and include many stretches. Don't be satisfied with just oil. Ask for a deep-tissue massage from an expert, a man or woman – fine, a woman – that has studied the body structure and muscular system. A good massage needs to touch you deeply. That way it will be effective in improving blood circulation and flexibility, and provide you with a feeling of nirvana, both physically and mentally.

If you're one of those people who don't like being touched, my condolences. There's nothing like touch. Every dog needs it. There are different types of massages, from gentle stroking with oil to being beaten in a steam room (straw lashes and rich foam). During a massage, lie naked. Don't worry, she's seen plenty of naked backsides in her life. Besides, she's going to cover you with a towel. In any case, relax and enjoy. A man needs to know how to give in. This is a good opportunity to practice. One last thing: before the massage, have a shower. Of course, do the same thing afterwards.

EPILOGUE

There was a time when I played beach volleyball in Santa Monica. We were a group of men, every Saturday afternoon, meeting to display our masculinity. Under the cover of exercise, we would attract admiring glances from dozens of young women examining our chiseled bodies. Leaping at a ball when your feet are in the sand requires excellent fitness. Persistence in the sport helps build the triangular body of magazines. We had ambition, we ate properly, we swam in the ocean, and we saw results.

Flat stomach, six-pack, broad shoulders, tight butt. That was Paul, one of the guys. A good player with a great physique. Paul was a bachelor at heart, liked girls, liked to party. He used to arrive at a game after a "Paul Night" – a long night that included lots of alcohol, Paul, and his girl of the month. We used to complain that he came after a workout while we just came after breakfast.

By the end of the game, another girl would have fallen into his net, impressed by his game of beach volleyball. Until Elizabeth. It's a long story, but at the end, Paul fell into her net. When Elizabeth decided that she didn't want to be another one of those women, Paul started showing up late to our games. When he did arrive, he would complain that he was full from a meal at her parents' place.

Gradually, he began to show up for games once every two or three weeks. The climax came after one month, with twenty extra pounds. We suggested that maybe we should play sitting down. He didn't laugh. Paul changed from a desirable bachelor to a guy who had messed up. He had lost his grace and charm. Finally, he stopped coming. Someone who bumped into him six months later said that he was hardly recognizable. Paul's story turned into a motto at volleyball: Every time one of the guys started dating someone seriously, we would say, "Just don't fall like Paul."

What do I want from you? If you meet someone, don't stop living the life you lived before. Make room for her, add her to your life, no problem. But don't forget your past. You had a good time before her, no? It turns out that you'll have an even better time now. Great. We're happy for you. But she should come to your beach volleyball games, and you shouldn't go to her parents. You loved volleyball? The guys were cool? You stayed in shape? So why stop? Don't act as though you've been married for thirty years when you're only thirty years old. It will come, trust me. Take your time.

By the way Paul, I heard you guys broke up. Come back and play.

WANT TO UNDRESS?

· ·

GET DRESSED!

Clothes have a special place of respect for me. They have a special place in my work. In one of the harder and more interesting exercises, we were asked to look at a lineup of ten people for two minutes, go for lunch, and then come back and describe as many of the people as possible and exactly what they wore. From this we learned the secret of unrecognizable attire. In work like mine, you need to dress in a way that is immediately forgettable. A pink tie and feathered straw hat – no way. If you want to blend in without raising interest, choose gray clothes, ones that are quiet and non-descript. An eyewitness will remember a long coat but not a short jacket. Trust me. But that belongs to the past, and chances are this isn't what you're worried about. You just want the women at the office to say, "That guy knows how to dress." I get it.

The rise of high-tech and start-up companies has legitimized plain clothing. Suits and ties are passé, an enslavement to anachronistic codes, part of white-collar slavery. Casual is the way to go. Good jeans, a good T-shirt, a pair of good low boots. Why the focus on good? Because in the clothes that I described, you can look drop-dead handsome or absolutely wretched.

Don't buy just any old pair of jeans. Look for the brand and style that's right for your body. If you have the thighs of a Sumo wrestler, don't wear skinny jeans. If you've got a small gut, go for a low waist. If your butt isn't sexy, buy a pair that's one size too big. Loose is always better. As for tops – T-shirts, shirts, sweatshirts, jackets, etc. – don't buy anything that's too small, even a bit too small. A man in a shirt that's too small looks like a midget wearing his son's clothes. Keep in mind that measurements are not an exact science. Every brand has its own inch. Millions of men are walking around in medium when they should be wearing large, and large when they should be wearing extra large.

UNDERWEAR

Men's underwear has two functions: comfort and impact. The impact is for her, but for you, too. As for comfort, underwear styles are determined by their cut. Jockstraps, briefs, trunks, boxer briefs, boxers. Men are usually quite set about their favorite style of underwear. I suggest trying a variety of styles, maybe you'll suddenly feel that you're ready to replace an old way of thinking. One fixation is the idea that briefs are uncomfortable. Briefs can be very comfortable because the movement of the thighs is freer. In fuller underwear such as boxers, the leg opening required for freedom of movement simply isn't there.

The most important thing is size. What size do you buy?

Medium? Most men think they are medium, but the problem is that manufacturers behave as though we are living in a world of dwarves. Sizes screw up everything. I wear a size thirty-two jeans, weigh one hundred seventy pounds, and have a pretty small butt. For years, I bought medium-sized underwear and suffered from underwear that was tight in the hips and balls. I moved to large. My life improved, but I still felt things weren't quite right. Only when I started wearing extra large did I find peace and tranquility. This is the size that's right for me, and after a few washes, everything is tight and well-packed. If I can go with an extra large, you and your medium are in trouble. This is the place, by the way, to tell you that it's time to stop letting your wife buy you underwear. You're not a baby and only you know how your balls feel. Go to the store and buy yourself the right size and style.

About impact. When a man takes off his pants, his underwear is the star. Underwear is for a man what a bra is for a woman. It's your business card. If you're hairy in the groin area or your thighs are nothing to write home about, wear boxers. There's something cool about boxers. Casual. Boxers show you've got confidence. A bit grunge. A young guy who's not afraid to look old. The minus – when you've got a hard on and you're not wearing underwear that wraps and packs your weapon close to your stomach, it looks like a stick in the middle of a tent. If you're in your first bed days with your woman, wear briefs – not a jockstrap. Briefs make you look chiseled, the sides of your thighs are pulled out forcefully, your butt is firmly packed and your dick fills most of the front part. It's not a jockstrap that shouts "Hey, I'm a gigolo."

Colors? Black. Gray. That's it. Black is best. I don't believe in red, blue or green. Save these for the T-shirt. As for white, it's possible, but you must be clean. Note that every drop of piss will leave its mark. I'm a clean sort of guy, but I still find that white is too clean. If you're a steady couple, go ahead and surprise her every couple of weeks with color, but if it's a one-night thing, or if it's the first night, black.

PANTS

Let's start with the classic mistake most men make. Shortening them. Most manufacturers make pants with a standard length of thirty-four inches. This means they don't have to produce too many options, but it also means that you probably have to shorten them. Usually, you stand in front of the seamstress, she pins the bottoms, the pants go out and when they come back, it turns out that they are too short. There are two reasons for this:

1. During the measuring, you pulled them down an inch lower than your waist.
2. You measured while standing, while in reality, you sit and your pants go up about two inches.

The result: Your pants are too short. When you sit in the living room or office, your entire shoe is exposed, along with the sock and sometimes part of your ankle, too. Very bad. Always shorten one inch less than the seamstress marks. Don't be wooed by her attempts to convince you otherwise. We've heard it all before. Remember: better too long than too short. Not to mention the fact that you can always shorten a bit more.

ORIGINAL HEM

Look at the hem of your pants, especially jeans. They have a designed finish, usually a nice seam that slightly thickens the end of the pant leg. It's known in the industry as the original hem. When you shorten your pants, all that design goes out the window, so remember to ask for the original hem. It takes some effort from the seamstress, but that's not your problem. If you don't ask, it will be a problem. Jeans without an original hem lose fifty percent of their cool.

SO WHAT TO WEAR?

It all depends on the nature of your job. I can't tell you to wear jeans if you're a senior bank clerk and bank policy forces you to look like a bank clerk. The bank wants its clients to feel that their money is in solid hands, and that's why they want your legs to look solid and gray. But you still have room to maneuver. Forget about your tailored wool pants. Look for stylish, comfortable cotton pants from brands like Dockers. Go into men's clothing stores, try on all types of styles – it doesn't cost anything. Ask the salesperson to show you options. Try them on, don't be lazy. A new world is opening up before you. Buy three different pairs, wear them and see how people react. Slowly, you'll find the best choice.

If you have to look presentable but still want to feel hip and charming, there's nothing like suit pants that are long and sleek, a well-fitted T-shirt and a matching light jacket. Leave the shirt out, no belt. If you're in an easygoing profession and have the freedom to wear whatever you want, there's nothing like jeans. They're a timeless classic, always in style. Not redneck jeans, by the way. The world of jeans has been revolutionized, and there are jeans today by a wide variety of designers in all sorts of styles. Modern jeans are appropriate almost any time and any place.

T-SHIRTS

Making a good T-shirt is a skill; choosing one is an art. Here, too, you need to find the right brand and style. The top seam should be one-half inch below the bottom of the neck. Not on the neck and not on the chest. The sleeves need to embrace the arms, not press on them so tight that they block the arteries, and not so loose that they flutter like a boat's flag in a storm. Long sleeves should reach the wrists, not cover them. When it comes to button-down shirts, I don't wear them anymore. I gave away the ones I had, and I had hundreds. I don't like the feel of them, and I'm not crazy about how they look, either. Tucked into pants, you look like a nerd, especially if you need a belt. In that case, you look like a super nerd. Outside the pants, it makes you look short and covers the nice part of the jeans. The lesser evil is a button-down shirt with jeans, with sleeve cuffs folded twice (just past the watch, about two inches).

So what is a yes? There are some possibilities. I prefer a good T-shirt with good jeans and some really nice shoes or boots. I emphasize "good" here, because there's a lot of unflattering junk in stores. What I mean is the shirt has to be the right size, from a good company and in the right color. The jeans should flatter you from the hips to the heels, according to your body type. I don't recommend a specific brand because it's really an individual thing, I just want to say that ever since Levi's came out with their classic 501s, brands have been creating amazing jeans.

In cool weather, I throw a jacket over my shirt. Forget about your dad's jackets. Today, there are some really nice jackets out there, leather, corduroy, cotton, so many different styles – patched, distressed, destroyed. My jackets are from brands like Armani and Boss, along with a few finds from unknown but excellent Italian, Spanish and American brands.

Sometimes, you may still have the urge to go out looking elegant. There's a winning formula. I learned it from the salespeople at the Armani store in London – classic black shoes, nice black trousers, a new black T-shirt that sits perfectly (not tucked in) and a tailored but cool black jacket. Every woman will be crazy about how you look. You can take off the jacket and look young, casual. Leave the jacket on, and look respectable but stylish and cool, someone who doesn't rely on anyone. Here's the trick: Go to the movies, look at the hero. If he's a not a senior banker, statesman, or the chairman of some company, he's not wearing a suit and tie. Scriptwriters want women to go crazy over him. Pay attention to the exact style. Try to remember or even take notes. Put them in your pocket, and you'll have a couple of role models.

Now, let's talk about shopping for a minute. First of all, look for a saleswoman. Many of the men who work in clothing stores are gay and if you leave the work of dressing in the hands of a gay man, there's a good chance you'll come out looking great to gay men. The question is, who do you want to look great for? If you're dressing for women, let a woman dress you. Let her dress you as though you are her man.

Look at the mannequins in the shop window. You'll see some good styles and outfits. Choose a mannequin whose look you like. Look at a store poster. In most cases, it features the store's best look. By the way, that's most true when it comes to sunglasses. There, everything is design and image. Look at the poster. On the face of the gorgeous model, they'll display the season's best sunglasses. Ask for them right away. Don't be surprised if they've run out. Anyone who has half a brain has already bought them.

Sunglasses, by the way, tend to get lost. Keep a pair in the car. Leave them there. When you get out of the car in the middle of the day, put them on, but at the end of the day, put them back in the glove compartment. Now I want to point out something critical. If your sunglasses are connected to a string and sometimes you take off the sunglasses and let them hang around your neck, you're in trouble. It's not sexy. Sunglass designers do everything they can to make you look good. A man with the right sunglasses looks great. If designers thought that having a string hanging from the glasses made anyone look better, they would have added it themselves. That string transforms a fashionable accessory into a donkey harness. Worse still – if your regular glasses are also hanging from a string around your neck, and you switch between the glasses when needed, you're a donkey and you're stuck.

SHOES

Everything starts with the shoes. When I go to meetings with new people, the first thing I do is check out their shoes. It's a habit from when I was in the service, but it works fine in civilian life, too. Let's say the man in front of you is pretending to be a wealthy businessman. He'll show up in a suit and tie, but two things will give him away: his shoes and his belt. These two items will be scuffed and faded, out of style and won't match his outfit. A belt is a matter for professionals, but the shoes will scream the truth. You can check my thesis in any casino. Gamblers must dress up because there's a dress code, but a look at their shoes reveals the truth. The man in the dark suit, his shoes are light khaki. Scuffed, stained, lost their original shape long ago and took on the shape of his clumsy foot. Boat shoes that became sinking ships, just like him. Anyone who needs a costume will rent a suit but stay in his own shoes.

Let me say this: If you have the money to buy just one item, don't think twice. Buy yourself a good pair of shoes. Don't scrimp. Wedding suits can be rented, but not shoes.

With jeans, I recommend shoes that don't have laces. Most recommended: low boots. Leave your high boots in Texas. Low boots give you good posture, make you a bit taller, are easy to put on and take off, and there are so many varieties to choose from. With dark blue jeans, I recommend dark brown boots. With light jeans, go for black.

Pointed boots are more masculine, and can be polished or rough. It's part of their charm. Sturdy boots may come with a zipper on the side. Soft leather boots need to be of good

quality, with a little rounded tip, well-kept and cared for. Such boots may come with an elastic side, and are essentially stylish designer shoes, just plain, without laces and covering the ankle. As for boat shoes, the problem with them is taste and understanding. Most boat shoes are awful. Few are the work of an expert designer. If you're not sure of your own sense of style, consult with someone. In any case, don't buy cheap boat shoes. They'll look like bloated kayaks within a month. And don't ever wear boat shoes without socks. It may look tempting, but it's a stinky, sticky trap. Remember that pair of socks you have in reserve. Go to a movie without first going home first? The least you can do is change your socks.

SWEATS

If you're not a style king and don't have incredible taste, it's best that you never wear a tracksuit. Ever. Sweatpants are rarely flattering. It's a matter of cut, design, fabric. It's not by chance that most people who wear tracksuits are not waiting for anyone. It's an article of clothing that fits somewhere between a hospital gown and pajamas and that final resting place that we're not going to think about. Nevertheless, there are some great tracksuits out there, mostly from companies that specialize in fashionable sportswear. There are also successful brands of jeans that make great exercise wear. Go to one of those stores and ask to see the styles. Try them on. Sweatpants don't need to be really tight, but they shouldn't look like a laundry bag, either. If you wear sweatpants, wear running shoes. Ideally, ones that are cool and not too wide. Don't ever wear sweats with sandals.

Most importantly: Don't ever wear a tracksuit with matching sweatpants and a sweatshirt. It's the insult of the century. If you're wearing sweatpants, wear a T-shirt. If you bump into a man wearing a tracksuit, walk away quickly. And while I'm already talking to you, I would say that you should also stay away from anyone wearing jean overalls, unless you're Angelina Jolie, in a movie about a woman who is painting her rented apartment.

ZORBA OR CHARLES

....

IT'S TIME TO DECIDE WHO YOU ARE, A GREEK GOD OR A BRITISH PRINCE. THIS WILL HELP YOU WITH BOTH WOMEN AND FISH.

Many women argue that you can know whether a man will be good in bed according to whether or not he likes seafood. There's something to that. We're not talking about the length of his dick or intercourse, we're talking about attitude. Approach to life. Libido. I've never liked men who compared a woman's vagina to fish. I was insulted for the women and for the fish. There's nothing like a vagina and nothing like fish. For men who don't like oral sex because there's something that disgusts them, I feel sorry for them. It's like not hugging your son because he's sticky from a lollipop. And then they still want a blow job, even though their balls are as sticky as the floor of a cab. In other words, it's about time you decide who you are – Zorba or Charles.

Why Zorba or Charles? We're talking about two different models of masculinity. The first is Zorba. You'll see him sitting at the port in Marseilles with his friends over fish soup. He cracks lobsters with his hands and sucks out their soft white flesh. He dips a slice of bread into the fish sauce and rinses it down with a glass of Pernod. You can also find him at the Caviar House in London's Heathrow airport. Jeans and a light jacket. His financial status may be better than that of Zorba in Marseilles, but both of them love life. In Heathrow, he sits over a bowl of mussels and a glass of white wine. He's happy to spend thirty pounds sterling on a meal, even though in another thirty minutes he'll be served a free one on the plane. He has style and passion, and isn't going to give them up for a reheated meal served on a plastic tray.

You can also meet him in a Greek village. At eleven o'clock in the morning, he devours a bowl of sardines with a glass of ouzo. You'll also see him at the market in Barcelona, in Tuscany, in Provence, on a yacht in Turkey feasting on lamb chops with a bottle of red wine. This man belongs to a cult. An instinctive and sensual cult. A man that loves to suck anything, especially life.

The other man is Charles. You'll find him at tourist restaurants. Usually he can't stand the thought of eating fish. He doesn't have any high culinary demands. Eating for him is about satisfying hunger. He would prefer to eat a simple steak with potatoes or rice, drink cola and have pudding for dessert. This type of man is more calculating, less adventurous. Less open to my taste of life. You could meet this man all over Europe, making a sour face, at the table next to Zorba.

Of course this is a generalization, but Zorba goes after the heart and passion while Charles pursues logic and viability. Who is more relatable to you? Ask a woman. Despite the financial temptation, most will prefer Zorba the Greek. Zorba will spend his last penny on a good meal and a warm woman. Prince Charles would turn his back on Diana, even if she was queen. Give me Diana and I will convert. Virtuous teacher by day, wild beast by night. Zorba will go down on a woman even if she's walked through the desert for a week because he understands that sex that isn't dirty just isn't sex. Charles will think eighty times if he should insert a finger or not, even if the princess has just come out of a dishwasher.

One of my friends, who owned several gas stations in the eastern United States, said that he thinks we are doing Charles an injustice. Charles was actually quite naughty, he says, and simply preferred Camilla to Diana. "Maybe," I said to him while we ate at a friend's house. "But if we could invite one of them to a meal – Zorba or Charles – who could hang out with us, laugh with us, and won't show up with a handkerchief in his jacket pocket, who would you invite? Who would you trust more if something happened and we needed help?"

"It depends on what type of help we needed," my friend replied. "Close a tab with sailors at a bar or get a passport from an enemy country."

***

It doesn't matter who you want to be, a Greek god or a British prince, when it comes to food, you need to understand. It will help you understand something about the taste of life. Food is an existential and eternal pleasure, and it's always available.

Pleasure in food attests to passion. Food can be the cauldron for heating up your relationship with your spouse. Cooking is easy. Three cookbooks, a few games in the kitchen, and you're an amateur cook. We'll get to it. Feed her – with a fork, with your hand, with a piece of toast that you serve her. It indicates intimacy and caring. It's romantic and sensual. Serving from a common dish is a great chance for building your future together. A few iron rules:

In restaurants, give her the better seat. Don't sit like an old man at McDonald's. Connect with the hostess, the waitress, the shift manager or whoever else is in charge of things so that you come out satisfied. Go into the kitchen and compliment the chef. Show interest. Tell them to send something tasty to the table.

Don't eat too much. I have a tradition with my wife. We order two appetizers and a single entree to share. Sometimes three appetizers. It's a great system. Varied, together, and not so much that you overeat.

At home, when you prepare food, open a bottle of wine (for instructions, see the chapter about wine). Forget about large meals at set times. Surprise her at midnight with a thin liver pâté sandwich and a glass of cognac. I promise, afterwards you'll fall asleep with a smile.

When it comes to breakfast on the weekend, don't hesitate to open a bottle of champagne. It doesn't have to be expensive. Pour a bit of Crème de Cassis into the glass first, it's called a "Kir Royale." A slice of salmon with lemon and your breakfast looks just like the one Bradley Cooper is having.

***

We'll get to home cooking in a minute, but first I want you to specialize on a different front. It's important to me that you become an expert in fish and shellfish. Not just because you probably understand regular things as much as everyone else, but mainly because your woman will be very impressed. You don't have to tell her where you got this information from. For all I care, you can tell her that you worked on a fishing boat in Alaska. A basic note: Fish is eaten in a fish restaurant. Not in restaurants that serve everything along with fish. Restaurants that you know, the kind where the chef has been living and breathing the sea since he was a boy. There's no shortage of them, everywhere in the world. You can identify them without having to know the chef. You can identify them after you know the fish.

HOW TO CHOOSE FRESH FISH
The gills – Lift the gills beside the head of the fish. They should be bright red. If the color is too dark or too bright, it's a sign that the fish isn't fresh. Second, the gills should spread like an accordion. If they are stuck together – not fresh.

The fish eyes should be transparent, taut, clean and convex. The pupils should be sharp and clear. If they aren't, don't buy.

Feel free to touch. Press the middle of the fish. The indent should return to its original place immediately. If it doesn't, it's not fresh.

Whether you're choosing a fish in the market or from the daily catch at a seaside restaurant, note all of these things. In the market, don't be swayed by talk about "the fishing boat that just unloaded its catch." These are tricks by fishermen who came back from sea last winter. In a restaurant, ask to see the fish before it's prepared. Check it according to the guidelines above. Employees will be impressed by your understanding, just don't go overboard. If it's a serious restaurant with certificates, you have nothing to worry about.

Shellfish are a more sensitive story, but no less worthwhile. It may turn out that shellfish aren't your favorite dish. If I were you, I wouldn't give up. I would try to crack the mystery of the magical oyster. It's enough to try it with the right guide and the secret is yours. It's true that an oyster's appearance and texture can be a bit threatening. The taste of the oyster isn't obvious either, and does require some effort. But give me an hour in a good oyster bar and I'd be able to change your mind. Okay, let's be fair. Out of ten people, I'd succeed with seven.

Clearly, there's a psychological aspect to all of this. It's not by chance that some men giggle at the sight of an oyster. It reminds them of a vagina. I think this shows their childish attitude toward the female organ. It's worth remembering that oysters are the peak of food luxury. It's no coincidence that the oyster is considered to be an aphrodisiac. Anyway, I'm interested in one thing at the moment. Let's say you love oysters and your girlfriend doesn't. What do you do?

1. Don't care.
2. Try a bit to convince her and then leave her alone.
3. Decide that you are going to make her love oysters.

I am one of those men who chooses the third option. In my opinion, it's one of the secrets. You know something wonderful, why not work hard until your partner enjoys it too?

So, how do you move her to switch sides, you ask. Good. I like it. First of all, choose a place that specializes in oysters. One of my favorites is the Oyster Bar in London's Chelsea neighborhood. There, and anywhere else in the world with the same amount of class, I recommend choosing the right oyster for beginners; that is, smaller oysters with a delicate texture. Start with a suitable bottle of wine – champagne or Chablis, or maybe Gewurztraminer, whose bold flavor balances the oysters. A refreshing and crisp champagne allows the oyster to slide harmoniously. By the way, you can also tell her that the fact that champagne, the queen of wines, goes so wonderfully with oysters proves their natural status as the shellfish that sits at the summit of culinary delights.

It's best if you prepare the oyster for her. After looking at all the oysters that have been served, choose the small, flat ones, with the least problematic texture. Separate the oyster meat from the base of the shell, drip on it two drops of lemon juice, a flat teaspoon of wine vinegar with finely chopped shallots, and a drop of red tabasco sauce. Pour a glass of wine for her and serve the detached oyster to her mouth while it's still resting in its shell. It's not a bad idea to immediately serve her a piece of toast with Dutch butter to help with the bite.

A small smile. The devil's not so bad after all. Now don't bother her. She doesn't have to eat another one. No need to weigh her down the first time. You can go back to it in two weeks. You need to continue working on it. Stick to it. She mustn't try herself and have a bad experience with an oyster that's too fat or one that is more suitable to advanced eaters. We're likely to lose her. You need to be by her side a few times, until she gains confidence. Until the taste grows on her. Until she is addicted. If you behave this way with everything, she'll become addicted to you, too.

THE SIXTH SENSE

· ·

AND THE DIAMONDS WINK IN CYPRUS

We practiced this many times. You go into the room. Everything looks normal. Go and find what isn't. In a room that's supposed to have been empty for a week, an analog clock shows the right time. There's no mechanical clock that continues to work after forty-eight hours. Someone was here. Turned on the TV, watched the channel it is set on. That's what the person who was here saw. What did they think at that moment? That's how you know if the housekeeper was here watching her soap opera in your room.

Or a police officer arrives to fill in the report. You leave the café in a sprint, saying, "I stopped for a moment to put something in the room." If he had touched the top of the car hood, he would have noticed that the car is cool and you're making it up. You'd been there for an hour, at least.

Or a pair of tourists, a man and a woman, arrive at the hotel to check in. As befits tourists, they come with two suitcases. They put them down and sign in. Afterwards, the woman lifts the suitcase. There's no gentle bending of the body toward the side, only the hand. The suitcase is empty. She's the woman you're looking for.

Again, you scan the room, looking for information. A man was supposed to be living in the room. A woman was supposed to join him and then they were supposed to leave and not come back. Did they already leave, or have they not yet arrived? In the ashtray, there are cigarette butts. If there are two types, the picture is clear. Even a child can understand. But let's say all the butts are from the same brand of cigarettes. Examine how the cigarettes were stubbed out and the length of the butts. If you spot two different ways of stubbing, bingo. Women usually stub out their cigarettes gently; men tend to smash their cigarettes, sometimes even folding them in half. Women leave longer butts. Lipstick is a no-brainer, and no agent was born yesterday, but touch the filters. Hers will be greasier and stickier.

Did someone pay the receptionist a few pounds to let him scan your room? Pull a hair from your head, put some spit on it and attach it to the closet doors. It should still be there at night. If not, get out quickly. Do this on a few openings, just to make sure.

A gray car is parked near your office. Evening. Dark. Chilly. You're on the sixth floor. Is there someone in the car? He's probably tempted to leave the car running and the heat on. Look for the exhaust pipe. Steam would be coming out of it.

We talked about sharp senses and the importance of observation. There's a difference between seeing and observing. If you're alone, you develop a certain kind of listening. To yourself and the world. You don't just see more, you see in advance. A moment before everyone else. Some sign will give an indication about an event that is about to happen. As for the event, everyone will see it. When I'm driving, I notice the problem before the driver in front of me. I won't get stuck behind him the way he got stuck behind the car that stopped. I'll change lanes before him, even though I was behind him. That's why I don't drive behind cars that have a curtain on the rear window. I need to see what's happening ahead.

Which reminds me of that story with the diamonds.

***

Winter '94. The scene: Cyprus. A small island that is like one big bar where everyone is either an agent, a double agent or a triple one. Because everyone is suspicious, no one is more suspicious than anyone else. The information was interesting. Agents from the former Soviet Union are trying to sell non-conventional weapons to the Iranians in order to transfer them to the Hezbollah. The Hezbollah is financed by the Iranians, who see it as a front-line arm to controlling Lebanon and a bridgehead against Israel. The information was about a bunch of these agents wandering around Larnaka, making shady deals to prove their seriousness. We wanted to get our hands on them.

We arrived in Larnaka, Belgian diamond traders with ten kilograms of rare diamonds. M., an Israeli diamond dealer, started a rumor that we had diamonds worth millions of dollars in our hands and were interested in getting rid of them at half price. Peter found us. A British spy who had been fired because of his affinity for drugs and gambling. Found himself a local beauty and settled on the island. Traded anything that moved and allowed for a nice commission.

For him, the deal was complex. We'd get the money, but half of it would be in drugs. Cocaine. Our clients, two Pakistanis, were interested in diamonds, but wanted to get rid of cocaine from a previous deal. That's the mess of the Mediterranean basin. Commodities and ideas switch hands on the way to the big and important deals.

We met at an anonymous fish restaurant. Sat alone on the second floor. Nobody believed anybody. We brought along someone who understood drugs to make sure it was good stuff. They brought along a diamond expert. When you sell at half price, the first suspicion is that the goods are fake. The scene was surreal. Between fish trays and glasses of ouzo, one guy is tasting cocaine while the other is examining diamonds.

Our diamonds passed the test. The cocaine, too. We closed a price. We drove to the hotel. We stored the diamonds and cocaine in a special safe room that had been assigned to us. Two separate safes. Each side received one key. Two keys were needed to open the room.

We all moved to the bar. Cigars and whiskey. Spirits were high. Women, politics, international intrigues. It's a dirty job but somebody has to do it. We left at midnight and arranged to meet the next morning at 8:30 a.m. Their flight was set for two hours later.

The next morning in the safe room, we turned both keys at the same time and each side took his own suitcase. The Pakistanis went to the airport. A private jet was waiting for them at the end of the runway. There was one thing they didn't take into account. At 3:30 a.m., one of the world's best safe crackers, a dear man who arrived on a night flight from Madrid, broke into the safe room where our suitcases were stored. He switched the suitcases. Everything looked exactly the same, except for one small difference. The new suitcase contained fake diamonds.

9:45 a.m. Our Pakistani friends walked toward passport control. The customs officer in Cyprus received an anonymous phone call: two foreigners were leaving the country with stolen diamonds worth tens of millions of dollars. Three customs personnel stopped the Pakistanis. Diamonds were discovered in the suitcases. The Pakistanis were detained. The (fake) diamonds, confiscated.

A British lawyer (our man, what did you expect?) comes to bail them out. He makes them an offer they can't refuse: immediate release and exit from Cyprus with the diamonds in exchange for giving us full details about our friends, the KGB agents. Who, how many, why, when, where. The Pakistanis had no choice. They talked with the lawyer. An hour later, they boarded the plane. We had everything we wanted in our hands. In their hands, there was a suitcase filled with fake diamonds. The customs officer in Cyprus rubbed his hands with pleasure. His part in the plan – a ten-carat diamond. Essentially, all he did was release people who didn't actually need to be stopped anyway.

To this day, we wonder if he knows that his lover's diamond is a fake.

BOND IN LONDON

....

BEING COOL OVERSEAS

In Rome, I buy incredible prosciutto. In Vienna, I drink cappuccino with mocha raclette. In London, I sit in Michelin-rated oyster bars. In New York, I hang around dark bars in the East Village. Okay, I also sleep at the Mercer Hotel in Soho. I'm not a kid anymore. In Barcelona there's an amazing tapas bar, I can't remember its name. In Istanbul, I buy carpets. In Paris, I sit at L'atelier de Robuchon. In Tel Aviv, I stay up all night. So do the Israelis. There are thousands of places, and every one of them is open. I have no idea if anyone works in that city. In Tokyo, I'm at the Hyatt, finding lost people in Tokyo. In Marseilles, I eat fish soup with local fishermen. In Turkey, there are incredible sailing bays. In Lisbon, oh Lisbon, the most talked about city in the world, there are terrific restaurants with seafood straight from the Atlantic and excellent wines at reasonable prices.

I'm not a tour guide and I definitely won't tell you how to see Europe in seventeen days. I remind you that we are here to make you amazing. Okay?

THE DRIVER

A driver should be waiting for you with your name on a sign when you arrive at the airport. It's not complicated to organize. It costs a few bucks more than a regular taxi, and is worth every penny. Someone is waiting for you. You won't have to wait in the rain for a taxi. Not to mention taxi strikes. Someone who'll tell you what's going on in the city, where's the best show. Ask him to bring your tickets to the hotel. Give him a good tip. It's nothing compared to the cost of the entire trip. Take his phone number and you already have a guide to the city.

UPGRADE

You arrive at the hotel. Immediately tell the concierge that you want to see the room before you bring up the suitcases. The clerk will understand that he's not dealing with someone who'll eat just any old meatball, and give you a reasonable room. If the room doesn't look good to you, ask about upgrading. It might be worth it to add a few bucks. Give the concierge a nice tip, too. You'll be needing him.

THE BARTENDER, THE WAITER AND THE REST

Leave the suitcases. Go down to the bar with her. There's nothing like a small drink to start a vacation. At the bar, pay attention to the older bartender. He's seen and heard everything. Take interest in his well-being. Ask where he lives, about his family, and so on. He'll take care of you. He won't be the only one. Information about parties, escort services, drugs, whatever – the driver, the barman, the concierge, the doorman, even the hotel waiter – these are your people. You need to understand who knows about these things. Who you can trust. Ask freely: "Do you know the city?" He'll answer: "What do you need?" You say: "Everything." From there, see how he responds.

BREAKFAST

In the morning, order a coffee with half a croissant to your room. I'm against breakfast. You're full and don't have energy. Have some cereal and be done with it. Walking around town with the top button of your jeans open on the first day is not acceptable.

HOTELS

You don't just choose a random hotel. I always choose the right hotels. The ones people talk about. Not because of their reputations. I'm just against walking for hours in an effort to see the entire city. Instead, you can sit and watch the city come to you. In the right hotels, the restaurant-bar is where everything happens. You go out for the night, come back at a reasonable hour, and your hotel is the hottest bar in the city. You can get to know people, drink yourself senseless, and then a simple ride in the elevator puts you in heaven.

Today, with booking.com, the world is at your fingertips (and often without any cancellation fees). Here are a few recommendations. And if you go, remember to send my regards to the barman. My main man in every hotel...

- Madrid – Only YOU, Unico, Villa Magna
- Lisbon – Tivoli, Lumiara, Fontecruz, Memo
- Berlin – Hotel de Rome, SO Berlin, Michelberger
- Hong Kong – The Upper House, Mandarin Oriental
- Barcelona – ABaC, The One
- Tel Aviv – The Norman, Hotel Montefiore, The Drisco, The Ritz-Carlton (Herzliya)
- Florence – Gallery Art Hotel, J.K. Place, Velonas Jungle
- New York City – The NoMad, EDITION, The Mark Hotel, Crosby Street Hotel, The Bowery, The Ritz-Carlton, The Mercer, Andaz Wallstreet, The Benjamin, The Bowery
- Los Angeles – The Peninsula Beverly Hills, Shade Hotel, Surfrider Beach, The Native Hotel, The Beverly Hills Hotel
- Chicago – Langham
- Athens – Njv, Grand Bretage
- Amsterdam – Jaz Amsterdam, Zoku Amsterdam, Conservatorium Hotel, The Dylan, Andaz
- Sydney – Park Hyatt, Old Clare Hotel, Ovolo 1888
- Paris – Buddha Bar Hotel, Hotel Daniel, Hotel Chavanel, Le Cinq Codet, Excelsior
- Vienna – Park Hyatt, Do & Co, Sans Souci, Guesthouse
- Zurich – Widder, Park Hyatt, Baur au Lac
- Rome – Majestic, De russie, JK Place
- London – Ham Yard Hotel, The Arch, Charlotte Street Hotel, The Beaumont
- Moscow – Ritz Carlton
- Copenhagen – Nimb Hotel, Hotel D'angleterre
- Oslo – The Thief
- Iceland – 101 Hotel, Vic, The Retreat, Hotel Borg, Apotek

- San Francisco – The Battery, Four Seasons, Hyatt Regency
- Prague – BoHo
- Milan – VIU
- Edinburgh – Scotsman, The Balmoral, Radisson Collection

PLANNING

Plan where and when in advance. Again, I prefer a local bistro or wine bar for lunch. It's enough to have a glass of wine with some grilled goose. Or prosciutto, pasta and grappa. Or beer with a medium steak to share. Okay, with a green salad. You don't need eight dishes and you don't need seven desserts. Go for small and high quality. Always. Think of a place that you like in your own country. Ask the young barman where your place is here. No need to look far. Don't waste your time. Think that a genius like you traveled across the city to sit five yards from where you are.

MUSEUMS

Not simple. So many myths, so much guilt. How could we have been to Paris without seeing the Louvre? Okay, listen. Find which museum has one of the best known pictures in the world. When I say "best known" I mean the Mona Lisa by Da Vinci or Michelangelo's Creation. Go to the museum and go straight to the floor where the picture is hanging. Find the masterpiece? Good. Sit across from it. Study it. This painting is worth a long look. It's worth fifty million dollars. Here's a short (partial) list of some of these paintings:

- Picasso – Guernica
- Claude Monet – Water Lilies
- Botticelli – The Birth of Venus
- Van Gogh – Shoes
- Marc Chagall – Paris through the Window
- Joan Miro – Cat Encircled by the Flight of a Bird
- Renoir – Luncheon of the Boating Party

Try to internalize the painting. Try to understand why it fascinates visitors and collectors. Does it do something to you? Talk with your wife about the picture. That conversation between the two of you is worth fifteen floors of walking through museums. Finished with the picture? Look for the museum's café. Your wife can go on a bit without you. You can make a few calls to the office, or reserve a spot at some trendy restaurant for the evening.

GALLERIES
Now this is something that I like. Galleries are usually located in cool areas. Off-beat areas that will obviously be the next hot spot. Cool cafés, artists and art dealers. The air is saturated with a combination of poverty and great wealth. Interesting. Galleries are usually one floor only. Not too much walking, and great possibility for interesting encounters.

SHOPPING
To be fair, I must admit that once upon a time, I was also caught in the loop. Slave to the idea that if you go on vacation, you must come back with a mountain of new clothes. You

run from one store to another, trying on clothes as though you were a tailor's dummy. At the end of it all, you discover that half of what you bought you don't even like. What's the madness? You'd think it was free.

The third day of your holiday will be for shopping. Wake up, grab a small coffee, and leave the hotel. To her surprise, a taxi and driver are waiting for you. The idea is simple: This driver will accompany you all day. He'll stop in front of the boutiques, you'll shop, throw your purchases into the cab and continue to the next address. No route required. Stop wherever you want. Browse. Nothing good? Continue onwards. The driver can double-park or drive around the block and come back in fifteen minutes. With the car, continue through the afternoon and more shopping. No need to drag around heavy bags and no need to return to the hotel after every purchase.

Right about now, you're probably thinking I'm some idiot who thinks you're a millionaire. So no. It's just a question of priorities. A driver and car can cost you about $180. Equivalent to one-and-a-quarter pairs of pants. Think about it. Together, you'll spend about $2000 on your shopping trip. Isn't it worth it to spend less than ten percent more on a car and driver? Isn't it worth it for her to think that you're the smartest, most generous, most indulgent man ever, a guy who knows how to get by? Most importantly, you took care of all the running around and shopping in a single day.

WHAT'S THE RUSH?

Tourists who come to New York City usually end up with a slipped disc, or sore muscles all over their bodies. All from wanting to see as much as possible. Relax. Here's a tip I enjoy: Stop once a day for a foot massage. Get a mani-pedi. You put your feet into a hot water bath, and let the soft, warm hands of an expert indulge you in pressing and massaging your feet with lotion. Nothing is more rejuvenating than this.

Beyond this, go slowly. Haste is of the devil, as the saying goes. Ask where the locals go. Where is the best market? What's the city's personality? When does the city come alive, and when are there only tourists in the streets? Where's the best local food? Clearly, in tourist towns like Venice, you have to go to the small restaurants where the locals go. Usually, these won't be along the main routes.

PARTIES

There are parties every day, especially from Thursday to Saturday. Ask the hotel to call one of the leading fashion magazines and say that they have a guest (your wife) who is a well-known model in her country, and that you very much want to drop by one of the popular parties. That they should leave her name at the entrance. There usually isn't any trouble getting into parties, as long as you don't make any mistakes. What does this mean? For example, if you and your woman dress poorly. Poorly means that you show up in black trousers with red Converse. A white T-shirt and a green jacket. On your neck, a shell necklace. Classiest is effortless black for both of you, with the ease of seasoned jet setters. You arrive in a cab that stops right in front of the door, and the moment you get out of the car, a cameraman pushes in front of you and shoots annoying flashbulbs in your face. You shield her and make movements with your hands that say get out of our way. The photographer is the young barman from the hotel (remember, the one you were nice to from the start?) who, for fifty bucks comes with you in the cab carrying your camera. By the way, this way you'll also have photos of the evening.

FINALE

Don't try to cram into the last day what you didn't have time for until then. Take your time. The best memory you're going to have from your vacation is sitting with her on a bench in Barcelona, drinking a glass of wine and gazing into each other's eyes. Take the trip to the airport in stride, too. Don't show up at the last minute. Check the suitcases and go to the bar. There's nothing to buy at the Duty Free. It's all nonsense. Spend the last half-day of your vacation calmly. Sit with a glass of wine and board the plane with the taste of vacation still on your tongue.

MAN AL DENTE

. . . .

GET THE RELATIONSHIP COOKING

You need to know how to cook. Don't worry. I'm here for you. I'm not going to write you a cookbook, and you don't need to be a professional chef. The most important thing is that we understand each other. You need to know how to cook because why in the world should you be dependent on her? And did you ever think about surprising her on a Saturday morning with a brunch that's straight out of the movies? A man who cooks is sexy. Cooking is courting. It's not by chance that chefs are the new rock stars. With a bit of help, you can be a culinary master in a moment.

First of all, I want you to have a private pantry. It's not a big deal. Here's what you need:

- Whole peppercorns, for grinding
- Rock salt, preferably Atlantic
- Dried chili pepper
- Dry mustard
- Excellent quality olive oil

- Fresh lemons
- Fresh garlic
- Onions
- Fresh tomatoes
- Canned tomatoes
- Eggplant
- Good bread, sliced and frozen
- Potatoes
- All types of pasta
- Raw tahini
- Rice
- Olives
- Capers
- Sardines
- Soya beans
- Nutmeg
- Fresh cilantro
- Curry
- Cumin
- Clam sauce
- Tabasco sauce
- Coconut milk
- Balsamic vinegar
- Vegetable, beef and fish stock, frozen in small portions

You should always have:

- 2 bottles of good red wine (keep in the refrigerator and remove an hour before serving)

- 2 bottles of white wine in the refrigerator
- 2 bottles of vodka in the freezer

Taken aback? Relax. It's no big deal.

TWO LIGHT APPETIZERS

Put some white cheese into a bowl. Add two tablespoons of olive oil, a pinch of salt and some black pepper. Mix well until you have a uniform paste. Take a ripe tomato and squeeze it over the cheese. Sprinkle with a bit of chopped rosemary or parsley. Toast two slices of egg bread until they are brown but not too crisp. Cut each slice into four triangles. Top generously with the cheese mixture. How hard was that?

Or how about this: Take two tomatoes and slice them into one-quarter-inch slices. Arrange the slices on a large white plate. Sprinkle with olive oil, add salt, pepper and a drop of balsamic vinegar. Place a spoon of the cheese dip you prepared on each tomato slice. What's the problem? Barely two minutes of preparation.

EGGS

How you want your eggs done is a basic question asked at every breakfast. Some tips:

Prepare the eggs at the end, when everything else is ready. I like to serve eggs straight from the frying pan so that they stay warm longer.

If you go for an omelet, add some milk and a drop of baking soda and whisk it all together. It will create a rich and airy texture. You can add anything else that you want to the whisked eggs. This is what's lovely about cooking – everything goes. I call it freestyling. For example: pieces of sausage, chopped tomatoes, chopped onions, parsley and spices.

For frying, I use olive oil and a drop of butter. A winning combination.

Before you add the eggs to the pan, you can fry all sorts of things, and only after about two or three minutes, add the eggs. First, sliced onions, on top of that, chopped tomatoes, on top of that, slices of prosciutto and at the end, the eggs. Delicious.

If the surface of the frying pan is small, cover the pan with a lid. This will prevent the eggs from burning on the outside while the inside stays raw. I know you're going to make a face, but put two drops of lemon juice on the omelet. Lemon enhances the taste.

I use organic eggs. They come from chickens that have not received hormones and antibiotics, and the yolk is a rich orange.

When it comes to sunny-side up eggs, many women don't like the yolk too liquid. Separate the yolk from the white. Place the yolk carefully in the frying pan. Give it a minute and a half to cook, and then pour the egg white around it. Boom.

Her eggs – two eggs in boiling water. Place the eggs in cups, crack the tops. Place a teaspoon of real black caviar on top of each egg. Beside each egg, place a glass of Martini Bianco with crushed ice. That's all. Now you can tell her that Nicola called this dish "Sucking Eggs." And that's what she liked every morning.

Poached eggs – How romantic. In a wide pan with boiling water, and a drop of wine vinegar, carefully crack the egg. The egg won't mix into the water but cooks on top of it. Carefully remove the poached egg using a slotted spatula. This is also the base for the famed "Eggs Benedict." I won't ask you to prepare hollandaise sauce, but do place the egg on a piece of toast topped with mayonnaise mixed with chili, and on top of this, place a slice of smoked salmon, salt, pepper, a drop of lemon juice, and a thin slice of onion. Cream cheese on the side, topped with three capers. Robuchon couldn't do better.

PASTA

Pasta is for people like us. People who don't know anything but want the very best. Pasta is for people who believe in freestyle. I've won over hundreds of women (okay, maybe not hundreds, maybe five, but the main thing is the feeling) with the help of good noodles. It's unbelievable. Ten o'clock in the evening, after amazing sex (we'll get to that), and she indicates that she wants something more. She's already got everything she could want in bed, so what could she be talking about? Tell her to read something in bed while you come with me to the kitchen.

As I mentioned, you should have some pasta in the pantry at all times. It doesn't go bad, and will secure you some serious glory.

Don't be a sucker. Don't fail because of mediocre pasta. Always buy excellent pasta. Go for the dry pasta (there's fresh pasta too, but stay away from it) made by a recommended manufacturer, Italian if possible. There are many types of pastas. I prefer two: spaghetti size seven or penne, so that the sauce you prepare soaks into the tubes.

To boil pasta, you need a large, wide pot. A standard package of pasta has about one pound of noodles. I boil about one and a half gallons of mineral water. Add one tablespoon salt and one tablespoon oil to prevent the pasta from sticking.

After the water boils, throw in the pasta. Give it a bit of a push with a fork, so that it all fits in the pot. Play with the noodles a bit to make sure they don't stick.

Don't leave the pot and don't start talking on the phone. Good pasta is pasta that the Italians call "al dente," which means "to the tooth." It should be hard and not limp and soggy. Here's a sign: Take out one noodle, bite it in half, and look at the inside. At the center of the noodle, there should be a tiny white dot, as though it hasn't been cooked yet. Don't forget that the warm sauce you're going to add will give it another thirty seconds of cooking time. Remember that overcooked pasta is lost pasta. On the package, the correct cooking time for the pasta's width will be displayed, usually five-ten minutes.

Remove the pasta from the water and drain. Don't rinse. Transfer to a large serving dish, pour the sauce on top and mix well.

You can start preparing the sauce (see below) before the pasta is ready, but not too much in advance.

While preparing the pasta, drink a bit of light red wine as it cooks. Remember the lady waiting for you in bed? Bring her a glass, too.

Call her to the table only after everything is set and ready. Clean the tabletop and spread a tablecloth if you have one. Place the deep pasta dish on a large flat dish and set a spoon and fork on either side. Put a nice amount of pasta on her plate (about one cup) and then top with the sauce that you prepared. Mix lightly in front of her. Top with some freshly crushed black pepper and a couple drops of lemon juice. Grate a bit of fresh Parmesan on top.

Her first bite needs to be amazing. It's best if she comes to the table with her sexy underwear and a T-shirt, no bra, the T-shirt can be yours or hers, her hair in a messy bun on her head. Chauvinist? What did someone just spend an hour cooking for? Anyway, she looks good that way.

Now listen. There's no point in me writing dozens of recipes here. Buy a book with pasta sauce recipes, there are dozens of them. Take the recipes that include photos. That way you'll see how it's supposed to turn out, and be inspired. I'll tell you just this:

Usually, I start by frying some chopped garlic in olive oil. I add a bit of red chili. That's how I start. The smell alone gives me a sense of professionalism.

The most important thing is starting with good base for the tomato sauce. You can easily peel the tomatoes if you soak them in boiling water for a minute first. In order to make sure that the peel comes off easily, make two small cuts in the peel.

My raw materials include tomatoes, garlic, chili, zucchini, eggplant, seafood (shrimp, calamari, clams), asparagus, lemons, and of course, fresh basil.

I'll list for you the names of some recommended dishes that are easy to prepare. Open a book, pour a glass of wine, and take life easy:

- Spaghetti with Lemon Sauce
- Aglio e Olio: Garlic and Olive Oil with Chili Pepper
- Spaghetti with Classic Tomato Sauce and Basil

- Spaghetti Frutti di Mare (Shrimp, Calamari, Clams)
- Spaghetti Zucchini
- Spaghetti with White Asparagus
- Arrabbiata – Spicy East Mediterranean Pasta

SPAGHETTI BELUGA

I had an Iranian girlfriend once. There was always caviar. This was our recipe: Heat a skillet over low heat. Melt two tablespoons of fine butter. Add a cup of sweet cream.

Add a quarter of a cup of vodka and a pinch of black pepper. Let it sizzle for a minute or two. Remove it from the heat.

In a pot, boil water for pasta and then add three quarters of a pound of pasta (about three quarters of a package). Remove the pasta from the heat one minute before the instructions on the package. Drain. Put it back in the pot over low heat. Add four tablespoons of caviar (doesn't need to be Beluga). Stir gently, without damaging the caviar. Divide the pasta evenly between two dishes.

Pour the sauce over top. Sprinkle another tablespoon of caviar on top of each dish. Pour some frozen vodka into two glasses. Bon appetit. Cheers.

SALADS AND SANDWICHES

There are some wonderful cookbooks with simple and excellent salads. I like Australia's Donna Hay and Britain's Jamie Oliver.

Goose and salmon: Take three pieces of toast and spread a thin layer of goose pâté on each of them. Place a slice of smoked salmon on each, with a thirty percent overlap. On top of this, arrange a few thin slices of fennel. Top with a few green leaves, primarily roquette. Spread some cream cheese on top. Generously top everything with lemon juice, olive oil, sea salt, black pepper and chili. Pour some chilled white wine into two tall glasses. Sit together and play with the dish. Afterwards, play with each other. Why not?

Salmon and champagne: The simplest, easiest, most success-ful, my favorite for Sunday mornings. On a long white serving dish, arrange half-inch wide slices of smoked salmon. Ground some black pepper on top, drizzle generously with fresh lem-on juice. Add a few thin strips of Bermuda onion. Place thin slices of toast along the side. Serve some chilled pink cham-pagne. Success in a moment. A bit expensive but who cares. Start living.

King's sandwich: Take two slices of good bread (rye, whole wheat, etc.) and rub some peeled garlic all over the slices. Spread a bit of mayonnaise or butter on each slice. Place a slice of ham, two slices of ripe tomato, a small branch of rosemary or basil. On everything, place a slice of fine Brie cheese. Sprinkle with salt and pepper, drizzle with olive oil. Turn the oven to grill, put in the bread, and grill. About three minutes. Serve with a glass of red wine. Wow.

SHRIMP URI

One day, after a hard week, I was stuck in Afghanistan. Tired, dirty, hungry. A friend (to whom America owes a hell of a lot) told me that there was a caravan not far away where we could have a shower and eat like kings. We got in the jeep and started driving. Two and a half hours later, we arrived. It turned out that in this caravan was a guy from Israel of all places, a cook who specialized in seafood. His name was Uri. We opened a bottle of tequila. I told him that I was once in Israel, that I had been a travel agent. Uri told me about his love for the sea and his love for Yael.

I fell asleep, dizzy from the tequila. I woke up an hour later to smells that I didn't recognize. It was the most comforting meal of my life. I asked him for the recipe. I told him that one day I would write a cookbook and add his dish. He laughed, shaking his long beard, and said that one day, he would write a book and tell about two suspicious Americans that dropped in on him one day from out of nowhere.

Here's the dish: Fry a juicy lemon, cut into thin slices, in two-thirds a cup of butter. Add a tablespoon of lemon juice, half a teaspoon of turmeric, one tablespoon of thyme and salt. In a large skillet, place two pounds of giant peeled crystal shrimp. Mix and remove. In salted water, cook eight artichoke hearts, peeled and attached to the stem. Make a bowl out of the artichokes and add to the frying pan with the butter and spices. Remove the artichoke bowls, fill with the shrimp mixture (along with all the liquids), sprinkle chopped mint on top and serve.

One of the best dishes that I have ever eaten. If you live in Israel, send my warm regards to Uri. Tell him thanks for the fuel.

NO NEED

. . . .

CONVERSATIONS THAT START WITH "NEED" ARE A WARNING SIGN

There are stories about couples that are straight out of the movies. For example, he's a lifeguard and she's a lawyer. Wonderful. I wouldn't be surprised if in reality, though, she sues him while he's out surfing. Of course, if both of you are, say, in hi-tech, the internal codes are the same. When you say, "We have a presentation tomorrow for investors," she understands exactly why you're so stressed. But you don't need to have the same profession, nor do you need to have different professions in the same fields. There are strings that connect everything, even if they are transparent.

Let's say she's a screenwriter. He doesn't have to be a producer or a photographer or a director. But if he's an accountant that deals with one of the big studios, then he understands the world of talent and great wealth. He understands that everything starts with – sorry for the cliché – a good script, and then they'll have many common things to talk about.

Common worlds can also be partial. It would be pretty nice

if you have a weekly activity that you do together. Maybe wine tasting, maybe a yacht-sailing course, maybe going for a walk twice a week. You have something that belongs only to the two of you. It strengthens the connection. Adds quality time. You talk.

This talking, it's the most important thing that there is. There are many couples that simply exchange merchandise between themselves. They don't really talk, they just exchange words. Chores. What needs to be done, what the technician said, when is the parent-teacher meeting, where they're going for the weekend, what they are buying for Christmas.

Some couples seem to be talking. I call them the reporters:

The wife comes home from shopping, for example. She tells her husband that she met Joanna. Joanna told her that they went to a movie yesterday. After that, she wanted tomatoes but in the vegetable aisle they told her the tomatoes weren't ripe enough. She wanted to buy bottles of cola but the car was parked too far away and she didn't want to carry them. She learned that the store started baking bread. The order turned out to be very cheap. Fifty-seven dollars. As she left the mall, a boy on a bicycle slipped on some milk that had spilt and his mother started a fight with the supermarket manager accusing them of negligence. She noticed that the car is running out of gas.

Wonderful. Riveting. A conversation that really contributes to relationships. Couples whose conversations really go like this are couples that don't really have anything to talk about, and because silence is scary, they simple ramble on to each other every day.

Try this. Out of the one hundred percent of the time you

talk to each other, see how much of this talking is about the soul, about meaning. Deliberation, authentic sharing, thoughts about the two of you, about friends, the kids, or your parents, as opposed to the exchange of technical information, arrangements and chores. Check how many of the conversations start with the word "need." For example, we need to replace the curtains, we need to sign the kids up for classes, we need to pay the housekeeper, as opposed to conversations that start with "I thought that…" or "did you ever think that…" For example, I think that we don't spend enough time together. Did you ever think of living in another country?

Conversations that begin with "need" are an escape from intimacy. A burden on the soul. They give you the feeling that you are terribly busy, in which case, who has time for philosophy? If most of your spouse's sentences start with "need," take it as a warning sign. As much as this may sound exaggerated, to me it sounds like she is self-serving, troubled, emotionally unavailable, and sees you mainly as a sack that will contain all of her negative energy. It's disheartening to think this way I know, but start understanding that she can contain most of this "need" within herself and only sometimes share it with you.

In management, it's called, "Don't let your subordinates pass the monkey over you." Talk to her about it. Try to get out of the technical loop of life. A romantic dinner over a glass of wine is a great opportunity for a conversation. Don't waste the time on electric bills. Try this:

"Those earrings are really beautiful on you. On regular days, I just don't notice."

"Do you think you'll want to get old with me?"

"Let's break routine a bit. Maybe we'll learn tennis together? What about that trip to Mexico that we canceled last year. Maybe we'll go this summer?"

"How is that car of yours? Having fun with it? Maybe it's time for some other excitement?"

Try playing the game, "Who Would You Live With If You Had To Choose Someone That We Know?" Suddenly, you'll discover that Thomas is actually her favorite. You weren't even impressed by him. What does Thomas have that makes him her default? What caused her to reject John, who's not a bad guy at all?

***

Listen to her. Talking is first of all about listening. Women aren't looking for solutions, they are looking for someone to listen to them. That's the first thing. Solutions will come afterwards. For every problem, first talk about all the possible solutions. Think about all sorts of things, just don't misuse one thing: time. Time fixes everything. And usually, the problem solves itself over time.

Talk about what lies underneath the surface. She's angry about something. You can argue about it until the cows come home. Instead of that, talk to her what's been bothering her recently. Let's try to think about it together. Something at work? Sex? Friendships? In her personal development? Maybe in her self-confidence that suddenly disappeared? Maybe the crisis of turning thirty?

Talk about you. Are you happy? What would you like to be doing next year? Have you ever thought about switching professions? About learning how to drive race cars? About studying cinema? We don't have the money for it? Maybe there is some? Maybe it's worth it? Do you see yourself doing the same job for the rest of your life? At the same company? Are you satisfied with that? Talk about your friends, about your relationships with them. About your parents. The kids. Or by contrast, at what age do you see yourselves having kids? Who said we would have them at all?

Go out to restaurants. Simple ones. A bottle of wine and pasta. A few silences, a bit of rest, a few glances, and suddenly a topic pops up. Ask her, "How was your day?" That's fine. But once in a while, try to ask how her month was. Let her think about it. Important conclusions will come. And how was *your* month? Talk about it. Be interested. Ask, flatter. It can't be that you won't mention her new perfume. You can also tell her that you liked the shirts that she used to wear better. "What, really? I thought you didn't like them," she'll say, and she'll feel like she exists for you. Go together to buy her some clothes. You sit on the chair and she'll try things on. If you like something in particular, buy it. Whenever she wears it, you'll remember that you bought it together. Afterwards, have lunch together. A couple of stolen hours in the middle of life. And I'm not even talking about the stolen hours in the hotel.

Decide to go to a play, ballet, opera or rock show once a month. Go for a fun evening or something. When you bought the tickets, you didn't know what kind of mood you'd be in on the night of the show. It turns out that the play is on a day that you have a small crisis. The outing will force you to put aside the crisis and enable you to make up and have a good time together. A play or really good show is like an adrenaline rush to your hearts. New ideas will pop into your minds, and be a trigger for some activity or decision. After a good play or movie, no one wants to sleep, they want to live. To talk. To think. Together. It's the glue of a relationship. This togetherness will remind you why you are together.

There are also dangers. It might not be pleasant but this closeness is likely to flood you with the feeling that you have nothing to do together. Deal with it. Recognition, conversation, therapy, a new beginning. Something that's even more unpleasant is that it could lead you to separate. It's true, who knows. It won't be easy, but there could be benefits to this too. Maybe you saved yourself five wasted years? Five years that could be five amazing years with a new partner. And don't think, why didn't I leave ages ago? It could be that you simply weren't ready to open yourself up to the world. Frightening, isn't it? It's a lot more frightening to let life pass you buy.

Sorry about the cliché, but there is nothing more important than love. Whoever has it, knows. Whoever doesn't, doesn't know that he isn't alive. If you don't have love, don't think that's how life is. That's how it is for you, now, and you deserve to change it. It reminds me of all the women who thought that amazing orgasms were only in the movies until they had one themselves.

Within this whole psycho-spiritual process, there is one landmine that deserves an entire chapter. Go on, turn the page.

TWINKLINGS OF UNDERSTANDING

....

THE DIFFICULT CONVERSATION IS NOT FOR AMATEURS LISTEN, UNDERSTAND

There are all kinds of conversations between couples, but I am here to talk to you about the hardest one of all: a serious problem, dramatic argument, someone was really hurt, a major mistake, maybe even a catastrophe like discovering an affair. You enter disaster mode. Just from the sparks of fury, the curtains could catch fire. Of course, along the way you made tons of mistakes, and of course from the conversation itself, new problems were created (So! You slept with Susan, too! Good to know!). Of course, we're talking about things that it seems only a miracle could save you from, situations that demand an immediate and magic solution, what they used to call in ancient Greece "Deus ex machina," which means "god from the machine"; that is, a problem solved with the intervention of a god. So, that's the thing, it's not solved this way.

There are problems that don't need to be solved right away, situations that by definition, it's better not to do anything about, better to let time do its work. Time usually knows what to do, even when it doesn't seem that way. Even a complicated problem that threatens to destroy your lives is likely to be solved by time, and by the experience and wisdom that it brings with it. When you are exhausted from an argument and see no way out, take a break. A temporary strike. Let a few days pass and see how things work out. On the other hand, in order for it to pass and for time to be on your side, you must absorb a few rules that will help you pass through the hell of the difficult conversation.

Women want to be heard. So basic, so simple. We talked about this in the previous chapter. When your spouse expresses distress, don't suggest practical solutions right away. The fact that you're used to saving her and the world, that you study and immediately see a way to solve the problem, that doesn't mean you understand her. The fact that she isn't satisfied stems from the fact that before all else, she wants to feel that you deeply understand her distress. If you express empathy and understanding, half of the problem is already solved in her mind. By the way, this is the same way how she berates you about something and you walk around for days with your shoulders hunched, but she's already forgotten what happened. The most important thing is to release her stress. It doesn't mean she won't be happy to get help, but only in the next stage.

THE HORRORS OF THE NIGHT

Nighttime intensifies the drama. Every choked cry sounds like a heartbreaking lament. The darkness, exhaustion, and silence transform a silly quarrel into grounds for divorce. And it's clear, of course, that the more you tire and want to sleep, the more she'll start throwing punches like: "How can you sleep? We haven't talked all day! Do you plan on leaving it like this?!"

A trap. A small question thrown into the air. If you don't answer, you're mean and hurtful; if you do, you're in trouble, about to plunge into the never-ending back-and-forth of intelligence, sensitivity, bitterness, tensions and everything else that she doesn't like. Your head is spinning, your eyes are clouded, you're dying to hug the pillow and drop into serenity, and she, like a woodpecker, just doesn't stop. Every now and then, you turn to her side, shoot out an answer, go back to your side, and think it's over. There is silence from her side. You're almost asleep and then she starts again.

Your path here is simple. Sit up in bed, turn on the light. Take her hand in yours and say: "Listen, my love, I see that it's bothering you. To tell you the truth, me too. I'm exhausted and not focused. Let's get up in the morning, refreshed, and we'll talk about everything over a cup of coffee." If you're a real man and plant a kiss on her forehead, you've played it well.

GIVE HER SOMETHING

You can't win every argument. It seems like you've won or given in, but deep down, she's still uneasy. Again, she'll feel like you're analytical, maybe, but also a demagogue, a juggler of words, convinced of your righteousness, it doesn't really matter. Nothing happens if, every now and again, you tell her: "Listen, sweetie, I think that you were right and I wasn't sensitive to the problem, but I was hurt too. I'm sorry." Don't forget to seal it with a kiss.

There's a frustrating stage where each of you feels as though you've been wronged. You're both hurt, each one focused on the wrong done to them, and the result is paralysis. Each of you is too proud to bow your head and say, "Sorry, I was wrong, I apologize, I'm nothing without you." Instead, you move to the stage of nagging and bitterness. Believe me, I'm macho and quite proud, but listen, sometimes it's better to say you're sorry than suffer for two days.

PSYCHOLOGY

There are some really complicated cases, cases that require in-depth psychological analysis, cases in which deep angers float to the surface, and not necessarily in connection to the issue that's under debate. Try and think about what's bothering her under the surface. Talk to her in a paternal way. This doesn't mean you should be arrogant. Just be mature and try to suggest a broader view of things. Maybe you haven't been intimate for a couple of weeks already and she feels that you're not attracted to her? Maybe she has a problem at work? Maybe something in her self-confidence has been hurt? Maybe her new haircut isn't great, maybe yesterday you were a tad too excited about her new friend? Maybe you haven't done anything lately to share the common burden? And maybe she's having her period.

I don't want to sound like a jerk, but listen and listen closely: You need to know exactly when she's menstruating. Two days before, already start being gentler, or just give her space. If you can, do both at the same time. Women before they get their periods are like ticking time bombs. When their period finally arrives, the sand in their hourglass has already run out. They're not to blame, of course. Imagine that every month, your dick starts dripping blood and your head becomes filled with nonsense. Not pleasant.

A FLOWER THE NEXT DAY

Send her something the next morning – a small flower, a heart-shaped box of chocolates with a red ribbon. After all, the problem will show up in the evening again, so soften things up a bit if you can with some soft artillery.

SURVIVAL

. . . .

IT DOESN'T MATTER HOW MUCH YOU'VE PREPARED IN THE END, YOU'LL HAVE TO IMPROVISE

The decision to take down a target is never easy. Not for the decision maker and not for the executing agents. I can definitely say that in every one of the cases I know about, the decision was justified, in the interest of having a better, cleaner, safer world.

It was in Madrid. We knew that the target (Mad Man) was going to be staying at a certain hotel. We also knew what type of room he preferred. There were eight of them. We had to bug the room. MM was experienced and careful. In the past, we had already caught on to him, but the bastard checked in at noon, returned at night and simply changed rooms. The challenge was how to install a bug in each of the eight rooms, so that whatever room he gets, we're prepared. A few months earlier, we had planted one of our men in the hotel, in the room service department. The problem was, he was too good at his job and had been promoted to a more senior position.

We decided that the work of installing the device would be taken care of by me and Sheila, my "girlfriend": a pair of British tourists who want to choose a room for Sheila's pedantic parents, after a careful examination of the view, floor, furniture color, etc. The condition for installing the bug was speed. We developed a special method which we practiced in a hotel room that was booked at the same time by another couple. I managed to achieve an installation and removal time of two and a half minutes, in two places, one in the bathroom and the other in the closet above the air conditioning system.

***

The hotel assigned us a junior manager who did everything he could to please us. While he showed Sheila the view from the balcony, I could disappear for a moment. In the first three rooms, everything went smoothly. I even managed to reduce the installation time by twenty seconds. The problem occurred in the fourth room. The manager who was showing us around surprised me. It was sudden and quick. It was embarrassing and dangerous. He understood everything. There was no time to think. His hand moved toward his walkie-talkie. I exchanged a split-second glance with Sheila. We had no choice but to stun him with instant paralyzing gas spray.

It was 6:30 p.m. The man lay on the carpet. We went into emergency mode. We called the other couple's room. They informed the reception that the manager had passed out and that they had ordered an ambulance. The ambulance arrived within minutes. Our driver and nurse, who made up the other "couple" who had come with us, hurried to take away the manager. The nurse injected him with material that made his situation resemble some sort of medical attack, and they left. We wondered what to do with the man. I confess, we wondered whether we shouldn't just kill him. You never know what he'll remember and which faces he can identify. Why take a risk? After vacillating, we decided to leave him alive.

We needed time to go through all the rooms where the bug had been installed and remove them to make sure that we left no traces. One of the rooms was already occupied. Only after Sheila's bursting into tears about a diamond earring that she forgot in the room while she was looking at it were we allowed in. The atmosphere was tense. There were guests in the room and we had to improvise. I told them that a screwdriver in a light socket caused an electrical short and darkness. I took down the bug on the pretext of trying to fix the power failure. We got out. We disappeared from the city. We failed, but survived. It's a failure that's discussed often in training, and used as a base for learning and practice. The decision to keep the manager alive helped us recover mentally. We took down MM a year later. The same technique, but in Rome. There's nothing like Italians if you're looking for a lack of vigilance.

YOUR CLOSEST FRIEND

. . . .

TREATMENT BEGETS TREATMENT, THAT'S WHAT YOUR DICK IS TRYING TO TELL YOU

It's not easy to be the new guy. Listen to one catch and you'll understand the depth of the problem: Most women don't have orgasms from penetration. Instead, they have orgasms after clitoral stimulation. Nevertheless, a man is still measured for his ability to achieve a sustained erection and active penetration time. I don't envy him.

But let's do this in order. For young bachelors, it's easy to get laid. Women today are not prey; they are often predators. They are independent, free from old ideas, and know what they want. The concept of "giving it away" has lost its meaning. Instead, we talk about women being assertive or, when they are older, cougars. The pick-up bar has turned into an arena where the women choose the men. The man has become the easy lay, or if you prefer, the man is the new woman. The era of liberation that became sexual freedom has turned female passion into a consumer power, and men are one type of supplier.

Unfortunately, there are no privileges connected with the new male status as the object of woman's desire. A man still has to prove himself, as men had to in the past. Women don't have to worry about getting hard or not getting hard. They don't have to deal with early ejaculation (something which essentially ends the fuck) and they don't have the opposite problem either, that they can't have an orgasm. If a woman doesn't have an orgasm, she can still fake it, and if she doesn't fake it and doesn't have an orgasm, it's the man's "fault." The man is the one who is judged over whether the fuck was good or not good.

Here, the absurdity only increases. Since the first fuck is a kind of test for the man, especially if we're talking about short flings, it requires the man to reach his peak already on the first night. The excess pressure placed on the man can often bring about the opposite effect – mediocre performance in the best case, fear of failure and impotence in the worst. And we haven't even mentioned the fact that the modern man must be a romantic, a soft, sensitive and understanding lover.

***

The age of the independent woman confuses the man. He comes to bed after a day of work, tired, aware of his anxieties, strained by the professional and economic competition that reminds him every day that he hasn't yet reached self-realization, and that's without even talking about the 'exit'. Greed is stronger than ever, career measurement is stronger than ever, and sexuality is too. You are expected to live up to standards of machismo of the old world, standards that expect you to "fuck hard" and also of the new world, of connecting sexuality to your feminine side. The desire to satisfy, succeed and live up to all the expectations neglects the man, who also needs touch and pleasure in his own way. So, what do you do?

Forget about norms. Be connected to yourself. Don't be occupied with showing off your abilities, but with understanding yourself. Don't waste time and energy researching performance and don't feel obligated to prove yourself. Come clean, calm, remember the positive message that our time carries for you, which is that you must not relate to sex as though it is a war. You do not conquer and she is not conquered. You are two equal adults who are looking for common pleasure in each other's arms (or between your legs). I don't see anything wrong with not seeking penetration on the first night. Better that you should gain confidence and plan the right rhythm and touch. Listen to yourself and do what you want. Remember that you came to enjoy, not to prove yourself.

And don't fall into any traps that she sets for you. If she's in a competition for orgasms with her girlfriend, send her to the New York City marathon. If she attacks you like a predatory tiger, send her to the zoo. And if she thinks she's the lay of the century but sucks your dick like it's the eighteenth century, send her to the museum. Be generous and sensitive, but don't be a sucker. Those are the men who are replaced the most quickly.

***

Your dick. Let's talk about it. After all, that's why we're here. First of all, the issue of size. We'll never get away from that. There are bigger dicks than yours, that's for sure, but I have news for you: from your own view of your dick, it looks as small as possible. Look at it in the mirror – that's how you see your friend's dick – and it will already look bigger.

You should know that it's not only the size that differs from man to man. Every dick has its personality. There are dicks that are quite small when they are limp, but when they harden, there's a huge gap between their limp and hard sizes. And then there are dicks that look pretty big when they are limp, but when they are hard, they don't actually get much bigger. Guys who have the first type of dick will feel that when they are relaxed, they have small dicks, but the truth is that when dicks are hard, most of them reach a similar size. That's just one of the reasons why size doesn't really matter.

Much more important than size is the art of the fuck; that is, how you move, touch her, and respond to her body. The first key to success is a deep connection with your dick. You need to be his friend. You must not reject him or become frustrated with him. By contrast, you must love, respect and award him. I'm not joking. You are attached to him at levels that are too deep to understand and are simply unaware of how dependent he is on you. If you want something from him but the desire is not wholehearted, or if your head is elsewhere, don't be surprised if he doesn't rush to do your bidding. If you press him to work for a quick fix and that's all, then don't be surprised if both he and she don't pay any attention to you.

When I say that you have to be his friend, I mean that you

have to internalize the fact that you and him are life partners, in good and in bad, and that you're dealing with something that is very sensitive. He expects you to understand how he feels, and that you'll know how to be supportive and understanding. He expects a pat on the back. When he gives you the hint that he's not in the mood, he expects that you won't bother him. Do you talk to him? I do. Every time I take a piss, I ask how he is doing. "Hey, Johnny boy, what's up?" I ask, interested. Do you pay attention to him? Do you understand what's happening to him?

It won't hurt to throw a kind word or two toward him on an ordinary day, even more so if you and him are active. It's true that the relationship isn't one of equals. You are the king and rule without question. However, as your most loyal servant, you would be wise to remember that there are days when he is as strong as a lion, and days when he can hardly get out of bed. That's why your orgasm is also different, according to his mood. Generally, I think that you can trust him. He'll already figure out what you want. You need to feel that there is a dialogue between the two of you. That there is a relationship. During the great moments as well as during the moments you would rather forget. I toast to his life. You should too. Always remember the great burden that's been placed on him.

***

Two small notes:

Pubic hair – regarding the hair in area of the penis – I recommend trimming it. You don't need to shave it or cut it really short, but do trim it, just as you would trim the hair on your head. There's no reason to have a dense forest around your dick, it just makes it look smaller. Women prefer that the area around the dick and balls be relatively smooth. It's easier to lick, everything looks fresher. Think about how you feel about her pubic area. It's more or less the same thing.

Masturbating – it's like driving. You may one day find a terrific private driver that is both gorgeous and good at driving, but obviously need to know how to drive on your own. Once you've mastered the art of driving, you can you relax in the passenger seat and let your driver do the job. You'll find tips about it in one of the upcoming chapters. Regards to your dick; tell him that we talked about him today.

STEAK-STEAK

. . . .

ROASTED STEAK OR BAKED CHICKEN
SHE CHOOSES, YOU PREPARE

You're the hunter. That's how it's been since the dawn of history. It's true that modern men are sensitive, connected to their feminine side, and all that other crap, but you're still a man. Be grateful that you don't have to drag the lion into the cave anymore, but you do have to know how to prepare meat. At home, it's you and her. Maybe another couple. I'm not going to teach you how to prepare goulash or roast. I want you to know how to prepare steak. It takes five minutes. No big deal.

First of all, buy a cookbook about meat. In every country in the world, there's a local chef who has published a book about it. Before you get the book, here's a short guide.

ENTRECÔTE
The best cut of meat for steaks. Comes from the front part of the cow. Ideally, this cut of steak should weigh at least fourteen ounces. The level of doneness – medium.

SIRLOIN

An excellent cut from the back part of the cow. Level of doneness – rare (raw) to medium. Sirloin doesn't have a lot of fat, and so it's likely to dry out if roasted for too long.

BEEF FILLET

The safest steak in terms of preparation. Steak for women who are afraid of steak. A very soft cut. It's quite expensive because there is only about four pounds of fillet per cow. Recommended level of roasting – rare to medium-rare.

T-BONE

Both sirloin and fillet, with the bone between them. The bone is in a T shape, hence the name. Should weigh at least twenty-six ounces. Level of doneness – Rare to medium.

FLANK

From the back part of the cow. Suitable for marinating. Very popular in the US. Put a large piece over an open flame, slice, and top with marinade.

PREPARATION

Buy yourself a steak pan – a heavy iron skillet, preferable with a lined grill. Iron skillets hold heat well, which enables good dispersion. The steak won't burn on the outside while it stays raw on the inside. The grill gives it seared lines, like when steak is grilled on a BBQ, and these are sure to attract admiration.

Now, look. The French understood a simple secret. There's

nothing like steak, a green salad, and a glass of red wine. You can make this even better.

Evening. You bought four steaks on your way home. You arrive, open a bottle of red wine (Cabernet, Merlot, Shiraz – a wine with body and depth that's right for welcoming the evening, and the meat). You drink half a cup or so and jump in the shower. You say to her: "Supper is on me, just make a salad."

Leave the steaks on the counter. It's best to prepare them when they are at room temperature. Get out of the shower, put on a cool T-shirt and set the table (tablecloth, white plates, two glasses of wine, her salad, steak knives, forks. A small cloth placemat). On the main plates, put smaller plates. Ideally, prepare a small appetizer (not a big deal, see the chapter on cooking).

Pour her a glass of wine. Sit and nibble on the appetizer that you prepared. Now listen: The first bite you prepare, but you prepare it for her. On toast or on a fork, serve the first bite to her open mouth. It's fun, it's romantic, it's sexy, and she'll trust the person who feeds her.

Let her continue eating, and while the conversation flows, go and prepare the steaks. The best steak for this situation an an aged, high-quality fillet. Fillet is the most reliable cut of steak. She won't find herself struggling to chew a rubbery steak with texture like a shoe sole, unless you want to enter the Guinness Book of World Records as the only man who ever managed to screw up a fillet.

STEAK FILLET IN CREAM SAUCE

- Heat a skillet over high heat until it is really hot.
- Add two tablespoons of butter and melt.
- Place two steak fillets, each about twelve ounces, in the skillet.
- Crush some black pepper on top.
- Turn the steaks after two minutes and then top again with pepper.
- After another two minutes, take the steaks out of the skillet and place on a plate that you warmed in advance. (Place two plates in the oven beforehand and heat them while you're preparing the steaks.)
- In the skillet, which is back on the heat, add one and a half cups sweet cream, a half cup vodka and two tablespoons mustard.
- Mix the sauce, which includes what was left in the pan, with a wooden spoon. Don't let the sauce boil or bubble out of the pan.
- Reduce the heat and put the steaks back into the skillet. Turn them over and let them absorb some of the flavors.
- Transfer to the warmed plates. Pour the sauce over the steaks.

Now enjoy a glass of wine with her and tell her that is an Elisa fillet, or a Nicole fillet, or whatever you want.

If I were a woman, this is the man that I would be looking for. If she's not captivated by your charms, get rid of her. A woman who doesn't appreciate your effort isn't worth it. I'm serious. We'll talk about it.

STEAK FILLET IN RED WINE

- Heat a skillet until it is very hot.
- Melt some butter or add canola oil.
- Place the steaks in the skillet and fry for one and a half minutes on each side (grind some black pepper on each side).
- Remove the steaks.
- Pour into the empty skillet half a bottle of good red wine and half a cup of beef stock (you can buy readymade).
- Add salt and pepper.
- With a wooden spoon, stir the sauce until it absorbs (scrape the steak residue on the bottom of the skillet to add it to the sauce).
- Add two tablespoons of butter.
- Stir while cooking for another minute.
- Return the steaks to the skillet with the sauce and cook for another minute.
- Remove the steaks and transfer to plates.
- Top each steak with three tablespoons of sauce.
- Drink the wine that's left.

COUNT YOUR CHICKENS

Because there's literally no end to the number of ways you can prepare them. Surprise her or her friends and reap great returns. Chicken breast goes with everything. Just grab some confidence and you're a qualified chef. Any marinade that you can think of works. Marinate the chicken breasts, put them in a frying pan for a couple of minutes and you come out a king. Here's a few ideas:

- Garlic, white wine, olive oil, rosemary
- Lemon, pepper, olive oil
- Orange, butter, maple syrup
- Wine marsala
- Chili, olive oil

It's best to soak the chicken pieces overnight, but you can also throw it all together on the spot. What about throwing it together in the oven? Here, too, there is no end to the possibilities. Even when I had no idea what I was doing, I would surprise myself and my friends with out-of-this-world oven-roasted chicken. In this case, I highly recommend marinating the chicken overnight and baking it the next day.

A few key tips to remember:

- Place the chicken in the oven when it is room temperature and not straight from the refrigerator.
- Cover the chicken with aluminum foil.
- In the middle of the baking process, turn the chicken over.
- At the end of the baking process, remove the foil and let the chicken brown for a bit.

Now take this amazing recipe:

- Three sliced lemons
- One pickled lemon
- One cup olive oil
- One and a half cups white wine
- Some Bermuda onions

- Green and red chili peppers
- Salt and ground pepper
- One teaspoon green tabasco
- Sage and rosemary leaves
- Chopped mint and cilantro

Put everything in a food processor and process for about ten seconds. Take a whole chicken, or several chicken pieces, and spread the marinade over everything, inside and out. Put the chicken pieces into a resealable plastic bag and refrigerate for an entire day.

To prepare, remove the chicken from the refrigerator. Heat the oven to 350°F. Remove the chicken from the plastic bag, arrange it on a baking pan and cover it with aluminum foil. Let the chicken bake for about one hour. At the end, remove the aluminum foil, turn the oven to broil at 400°F, and broil for a few minutes, moving the chicken pieces around a bit. Transfer the chicken to a wooden serving dish, pour the sauce in the pan on top, and let everyone eat with their hands. You can also serve it with rice. I prefer serving with a plain green salad.

Alright. Enough about food. Don't forget, we want you slim. We have many plans on the way.

MY MONEY'S FROM THE BANK...
YEAH, WHATEVER

....

TIPS FOR USING YOUR MOBILE PHONE

The most advanced and useful device in the world today, the cell phone, is not allowed for our collection agents and field personnel. We're talking about the most dangerous trap for any secret agent. It's so simple nowadays to listen in, hack into voice and text messages, and worst of all, identify your location at any time. In short, not only have you been exposed, but you have also led the person who's following you straight to you, even if you managed to get away from him physically.

So how do we get by? That's a good question. Let's start from the beginning. The mobile phone has made life very comfortable, it's true, but also very nagging. On the one hand, you can relax on a hammock in the Caribbean and talk to your Aston Martin agent in London. On the other hand, while you're in the middle of a safari in Tanzania, you may get a call from your dentist's secretary to see if you want to move your appointment to later in the day.

The mobile phone is a like a small personal assistant. Alarm clock, calculator, camera, journal, to-do list, calendar. Use it all. I write lists and notes, and use the alarm clock. Why trust a hotel wake-up call? I also use the recording feature a lot. Ideas and thoughts for myself, and all sorts of things I want to remember.

Here is the place for my first important tip: Many people use a lock screen to prevent accidental dialing. However, if you lose your device, your entire world may be exposed, so there are some people who lock their device with a code. The problem is, this requires a lot of work every time you want to release the phone from being locked. What can you do? Here's an idea: There's a function that allows you to lock the device remotely by dialing a specific code. If the device is lost or stolen, or even if the device is forgotten at a friend's house and you think he may snoop through your messages, simply dial that code and the device is locked. You just go through a short process when the device is with you and from that moment, you're safe. It's crucial.

SECRET CODES

All the secret numbers I need to remember are encoded on my cell phone. My ATM, credit card, home WiFi password, etc. Of course, I save them on my phone in a manner that's impossible to identify if my device falls into the wrong hands. You probably also do this, but I have a surprise for you: Give your phone to me, or to anyone I work with, and we'll crack the codes that matter in less than five minutes.

Do you think that if you write Monica Master + a mobile

number whose four last digits are those of your credit card, it won't be clear that we're talking about your ATM code? You're sophisticated but simplistic, and that's just not good enough. You need to be more creative. For example: Who doesn't have his father's number on their cell phone? And if you do, how about putting your credit card code under the name "Dad Office"? Let's assume the code is 3364, the number 65978434 will appear under "Dad Office". How does it work? Simple: write the code backwards (4633), added 1 to each digit (5744) and add a digit from the code after each digit in the make-believe phone number: 6-5-9-7-8-4-3-4. Kapish?

You may not need all of this for your ATM, as long as you understand the principal of code encryption. The main thing is names and definitions. If the code is for overseas, don't write Paris. If it's American Express, don't write America Ferrera. Don't list your ATM number under AJ or Adam. Always go for the simple, the stupid, the obvious. Audrey Nails is not bad at all.

And how does the name of the woman with whom you're having an affair appear? And what do you do with all the romantic messages you get? Erase them, huh? And how many times have you forgotten? Think about it.

***

The big thing about cell phones isn't fifth generation video calls. It's text messages. Text messages are the print of our generation, like pornographic literature is the oldest invention, since Adam and Eve, and it's alive and thriving to this day.

Today, mobile phone providers make big money from text messages and from the illicit romances that flourish there. The written word and distance make it possible to say things that we would never say face to face. Sexy messages stimulate the imagination in so many ways. Once upon a time, this was done with a feather, ink and paper. Today it's done with the mobile phone.

But herein lies the danger, too. The written word can knock you down, incriminate you, reveal your affair, and give proof of your participation in sin. It's enough for you to be excessively attached to your device or to respond with inexplicable nervousness whenever someone tries to look at it, to point to the fact that you have something to hide.

To be clear. I don't support affairs or long-term flings. Love is a precious thing. Love is based on trust. You can't get around that. Broken trust is like a broken pitcher, you can glue it back together, but it's not the same pitcher anymore. The fact that I'm giving you advice so that you don't get caught doesn't mean that I'm in favor. It just means I oppose negligence.

Make a habit of deleting all of your messages, even if you don't have to. You need to make it an automatic habit, like locking the car door. Same thing with incoming and outgoing calls. Always. Set an alarm for five minutes before you get home and it will remind you. Make sure that you also delete the last message that you wrote and that appears on the display. That's something people tend to forget. Also important: Delete both incoming and outgoing messages.

A small minefield is hiding in the call log. In the log of incoming calls, there's a list of calls, recipients and hours. No details about the conversation, but to avoid hearing: "Who the hell is Natalie, who you talked to when you were in Los Angeles at four in the morning?" Erase this entire list. Think that's everything? All set? Think again. Go to the message counter. You'll find there a small, incriminating little devil. Delete the counter. In some phones, incriminating evidence can be found there, too.

Now to the core. Take into account that at some point, you're likely to forget your phone at home. What happens then? Your mobile is at home and how are you supposed to know what message is going to show up when you're not there. Your lover's name is Susan. How should you write her name in your list of contacts? You can write "Susan Travel Agent" but why should her real name show up at all? You can invent a name for her and say that she's the secretary of someone you work with a lot. But how will you explain that message from her at an illogical time? The best solution is to give her a real name of someone that your spouse knows. Someone who writes to you and talks to you a lot. Someone who doesn't cause your wife to worry. Your nagging cousin, your partner at the clinic. I don't know who. If there's a message from her, your wife will be happy to let you know.

Another option is to give your mistress a man's name. Your broker, your lawyer. In order to differentiate between your real lawyer and your lover, add a letter or two. For example, the real one would be John and the lover would be Johnny. Suppose you're having dinner with friends and suddenly a message pops up. You're in the bathroom, the phone is on the table and your wife looks. "Your lawyer left a message," she'll report, bored.

Your lover must remember to start her messages with a predetermined code. For example: "The meeting with so and so is canceled." If you're free and the coast is clear, you can write her back and everything is as usual. If you don't write back, she'll understand that you're busy. How easy, how simple, how safe. Of course, you need to behave in the same manner. You must also write: "The meeting with the bank was delayed until next week." If she doesn't get back to you, it's a sign that her husband is beside her. If your wife sees this version of the message once, don't forget to change the code the next time.

Yes, you have to work if you want to cheat.

Being careful is also important for voice conversations. You need a plan in order to know for sure that the other side can talk freely. After all, if your wife is sitting beside you in the car and the conversation is taking place on the speaker, you can't say, "Oh, sorry, my wife is here so be careful with what you say..." So what do you do? Simple. Let's say your name is Timothy. Your lover calls and you answer. She says, "Hi Steve, how are you?" and you say, "Sorry, wrong number." Your lover will understand you're not alone, and you're as clean as snow in Vermont.

There's more. Let's say that in the middle of an illicit phone call, your wife comes into the yard and surprises you. She just came home. "No, I said I wasn't interested in subscribing to your newspaper," you say, using the code that indicates you're in trouble. Your lover answers, "Thanks and have a good day."

The agency has dozens of stories about agents who managed to convey messages creatively and by using codes when they were in danger or not alone. Every agent has code words that explain to the other side if he's in trouble or not telling the truth. Until we get to that, here's some food for thought: How can you know that it's really your lover writing you, and not her suspicious husband?

***

It was one of the hundreds of planning and improvisation exercises. Two couples competing against each other, and the clock, to see who can finish five tasks first (not simple at all). Each person was sometimes on their own, so the couples could proceed at the same time. The exercise included the right to paralyze the opponent. As a strategy, you had to decide whether to spend time trying to ruin the other couple's plans, or to try to achieve your own plans as quickly as possible. The first couple decided to paralyze the other couple. It was a Monday afternoon, at a time when the partners were working on their own, each person separated from their partner.

The woman in couple A wrote to the man in couple B: "I lost my device. I suspect they (the other couple) stole it. I am writing from a stranger's phone. Let's meet in twenty minutes on the rooftop of Harvey Nichols (a well-known department store in London also known as Harvey Nicks). Don't use your mobile device. If there's a ringing from my device, don't answer. I'll explain soon."

You, the reader, understand that these instructions prevent her partner from calling or answering his real partner and revealing the deception. The man reaches the roof of Harvey

Nicks, waits for his partner. At the same time, the London police receive a message that an anonymous man is on the roof of the store peeping into women's apartments. Three policemen come to the roof and find him. He tells them he is having an affair and is waiting for his lover to arrive. The policemen chuckle. A telescope hidden in a barrel on the roof (which the couple A had planted there earlier, of course) convinces the cops that they are dealing with a peeping tom.

Remember, even during drills, agents are not allowed to talk about their jobs. Only when your life is clearly in danger are you allowed to tell officials that you're an agent. And even then, there are many chances of you being rejected. In any case, if the couple had prepared codes for mobile identification in advance, this wouldn't have happened. Pure and simple.

THE RING AND THE CALL

You're in your car. Your lover calls. It's a time when you're usually alone in the car, but this time, your wife is beside you. On the caller display, you see exactly who is calling. What now? Anxious and confused, you hang up. Your wife is not a fool. She memorized the name and understands that she has to start looking into things. If you answer the call and start stuttering like an official from the Postal Authority and mention that your wife is beside you, it'll be crystal clear that something is going on. So what's the solution? Nothing is easier. Again, it's all about the code, this time during the conversation. If you answer, "Hi sweetie," then there is no problem, you are alone. If you answer "Yes..." or "Hello..." it's a sign that you aren't alone. She'll simply hang up.

THE EXTRA DEVICE

If you're having a serious affair, go ahead and invest in an extra device. Just for you and her. Talk on it for days on end. Write a million messages. The bill for that device will come to a different address. The device can be on you, concealed. The first time it's discovered, you can explain that someone forgot it at a meeting or something. Ideally, the device should not enter the home. Remember your car (your refuge)? It could be there.

Understand one thing: The length of the calls is also a factor. If your wife discovers through the call logs that you are having lots of long conversations with a single number, the story is over. Either your wife leaves, your lover does, or both. By the way, if your wife is having an affair and the bill reaches you, you can spot the difference according to the amount of the bill. If she is smart and is using an additional device, you'll be able to see that the bills are low.

Despite everything, and between you and me, it's better without stories, without codes and without affairs. You'll live longer and be more relaxed.

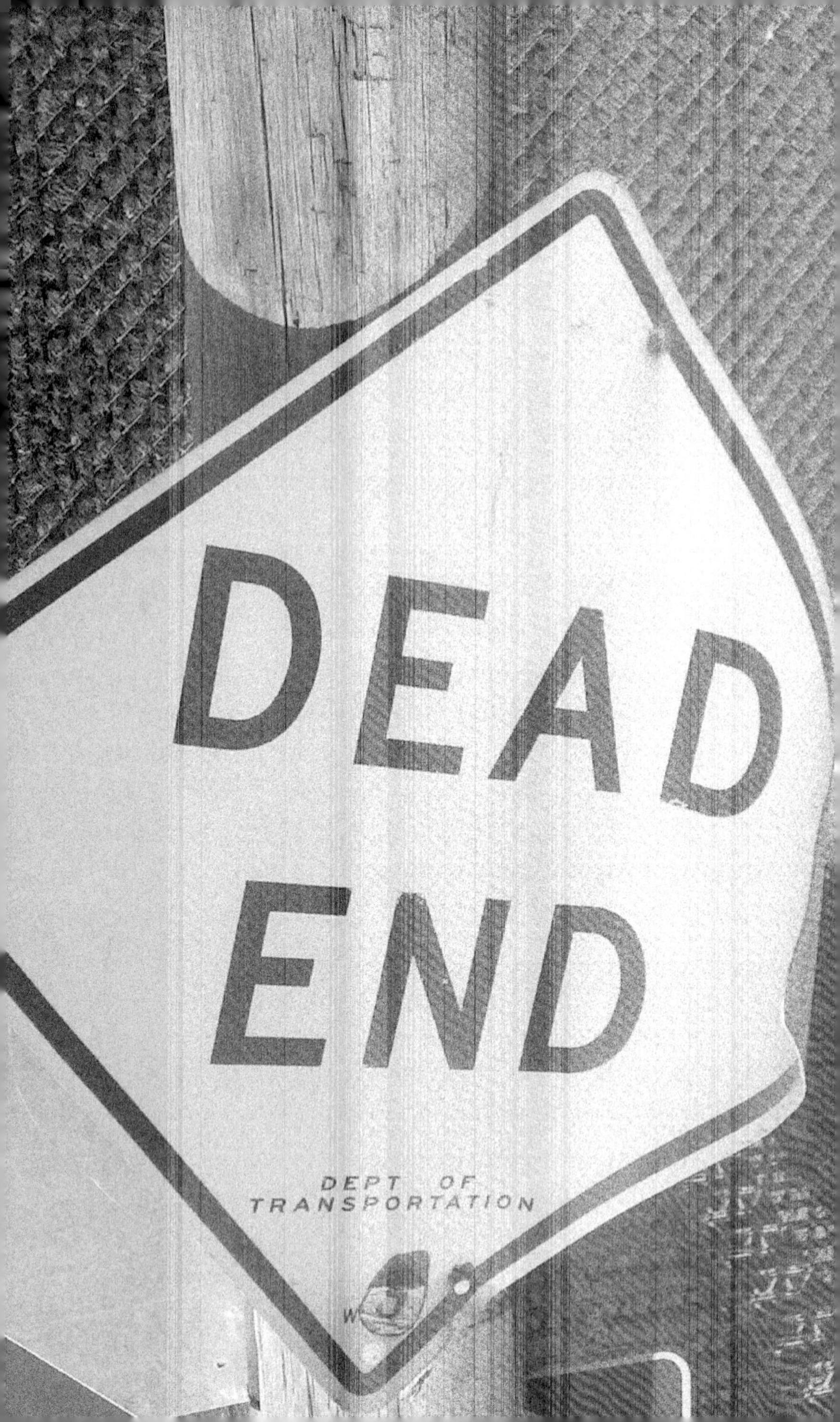
DEAD
END
DEPT OF
TRANSPORTATION

YOU, ME &
THE CAR THAT'S FOLLOWING US

··

HOW TO KNOW IF SOMEBODY IS FOLLOWING YOU, AND HOW TO GET AWAY FROM THEM

Men are like a small factories. They have a lot of suppliers; some permanent, some temporary. You start with something small and it becomes permanent: a dentist, gym, psychologist, masseuse, wine store, laundromat, dog groomer, barber, etc.

Of course, professionalism is more important than anything, but I suggest that you include another factor in your selections – proximity to home. At first, this may seem negligible, but over time, things turn out differently. My son needed to have his teeth straightened. We got a recommendation for the best orthodontist in the field. He was a bit far away, but I told myself that two or three trips wasn't going to kill me. I also thought I would use the trips for some quality time with my son. Slowly, it became clear that his treatment required many appointments. I found myself stuck spending so-called quality time in huge traffic jams. I was irritable, my son fell asleep, and we didn't gain anything from the experience.

Get an offer from a professional who isn't close to your home? Don't even think about it. This is even more true when it comes to psychologists. Weekly therapy is an important hour that requires relaxation both before and after. If nothing works out close to home, look for something close to the office. Also, check traffic patterns and set your appointment accordingly.

And if we're already talking traffic, I also set my regular work meetings according to traffic patterns. It's pretty dumb to set a regular meeting at noon with a client who is twenty minutes away, for one and a half hours, without taking into account the time. The same applies if you invite him to your office. Plan a time that takes traffic into consideration. A client who shows up irritable from traffic will be grumpy when he starts his meeting with you. In short, proximity to your home or office only *seems* like a luxury. It's actually super important.

A DISCREET MEETING

Men in the mafia used to meet in basements and restaurants owned by one of their members, or in saunas. The reason for meetings in saunas is that these meetings seem random and are impossible to record. Even if our colleagues from the FBI are following people from the underground, they can't install bugs in saunas because of the heat and moisture. Moreover, the meeting's participants are naked, with only a towel on their bodies, so they can't carry a recording device, either. If you're worried that someone you're going to meet wants to record you, arrange for the meeting to take place in a pool or sauna.

Where to arrange a discreet meeting? There are several options: under bridges, in abandoned parks, at diners that are popular among teenagers, car washes, etc. Anonymous and/or abandoned places that don't arouse suspicion. The best place we found was a dentist's waiting room. Except for two older women, it was always empty there. You immediately see anyone who enters the office, noise from the drill makes remote eavesdropping impossible, and you can talk freely.

If you can't find a suitable place, sometimes it's enough to get on a train and sit across from the person you want to talk with. It's hard to follow someone who buys a train ticket moments before the train departs. I assume that in your daily life, you don't need to meet with secret agents, but it doesn't hurt to know. For a rainy day.

ARE YOU BEING FOLLOWED?

Drive at a normal speed. Look in the mirror. Pay attention to the car behind you and behind it.

Stop at a gas station. Continue on and check if one of those cars is still behind you. Go into a parking garage and drive down to the bottom floor. Wait a couple of minutes and then drive up and out again. Look in the rear mirror to see if the car you saw earlier is still behind you. Try to also look at the cars that aren't in your lane, but are in the lanes on either side of you. Stop in a parking lot or at the side of the road. Go into some store and look out a window to see if a car stopped behind you or in front of you. Is the driver still in the car?

Leave and continue. Go into the parking lot of a large shopping center. Drive to the end of the parking lot. Try looking in the mirror to see who is behind you. Slowly leave the parking lot. If your fear increases, stop at a red light. When the light turns green, don't move. Wait for the light to turn yellow and immediately when it turns red, drive. The car behind you will be forced to drive through a full red light. Another way of taking advantage of a traffic light is to go into the left turn lane. When the light turns green, drive straight. You can also drive around a block of buildings. Right, right, right again. If you spot a car that you saw earlier, you're in trouble.

This is the time to shake off the car that's following you. At the next intersection, go into the left turn lane. Wait until there's just enough space for one car to turn. Turn. Drive quickly, and at the first opportunity, turn onto a side street. Turn off the lights. Wait a few minutes. By now, you must have succeeded in shaking off whoever was tailing you. Either that or you don't know how to drive.

A ROMANTIC ENCOUNTER

Once you're convinced no one is following you, drive to your meeting place. The meeting can be in any parking garage. Park on the lowest floor. Usually, there aren't too many vehicles there. She'll come by taxi. She'll get out of the taxi and go into the hair salon, coffee shop or pharmacy. From there, she'll go into the office building above the parking garage where you've parked. She'll take the elevator down to whatever floor you told her by telephone. Here, she's getting into the car.

If you planned to book a hotel room, don't choose some miserable motel. Choose a busy hotel with lots of action. Book the room in advance with a fake name. Go in and pay in cash.

Take the key. Leave the hotel. Go to a coffee shop. If someone is following you, you still haven't done anything wrong. An hour later, take an alternate route back to the hotel and go into the parking garage. From there, take the elevator up to the floor with your room. Let her know which room you're in. Tell her to arrive carefully, in some random route. On your way out, leave separately, a few minutes apart and from different places.

Complicated? Who said you should have an affair?

ME!

. . . .

IF YOU DON'T HAVE HIM,
YOU DON'T HAVE ANYTHING

When you ask people what's most important to them, you usually get answers connected to family, health, work, etc. Let me save some time – the most important thing to you is you. If you don't have yourself, you don't have anything. You need to live. For as long as possible and as well as possible. You need to get the most out of yourself and the best. You are the most important issue in your life. And the first, most important thing is to know yourself.

BODY

Go to a serious clinic and get a thorough physical examination. Go back every year. This way you'll have continuous monitoring that will measure changes in your health. Test your blood, heart, lungs, breathing, endurance, eyes, ears, blood pressure, pulse, and more. Depending on your age, there are also special tests for early discovery of diseases or growths. Once you're over the age of forty-five, get a colonoscopy to rule out colon cancer. Once every few years, go through more extensive heart tests. Medicine has greatly advanced in its ability to diagnose and detect. Prostate cancer sounds terrible, but if you find it early on, you can get out of it with relative ease.

Sit with an expert and go over all of your data. Know exactly what's going on and what you need to do to maintain or improve your health. Go to a nutritionist. Food is the body's fuel, but not just for regular driving. Also for long-term parking. Many diseases and problems stem from years of bad nutrition. A small tip: Apparently, the two healthiest things for the body are wheatgrass juice and umeboshi. These are canned, salted Japanese plums.

SOUL

Go to a psychologist. Yeah, I know. You don't have any problems. Dumbass. An hour a week with a psychologist is like having quality time with yourself. Every day, you talk to everyone, just not yourself. Slowly, with the psychologist, you'll find what you need to find. What you repress, what bothers you, what frightens you. After a long period of treatment, when a serious problem pops up at work or in your personal relationships, you'll have someone who knows you deeply. You.

Personally, I prefer female psychologists. My assumption is that a woman will also be able to see the picture from the other side. This is the opportunity to thank S.A. If it weren't for you, dear, chances are I would still be walking around the dark corridors of life at the CIA. Thank you, you have a big part in this book.

ABILITY

You were born with certain genes that are responsible for your skeleton. If you become a revered chess player or a serial killer, much of that comes from your genes. In other words, a lot was determined long before you came into this world. But not everything. Your childhood, education, parents and home shape the mental and psychological patterns that you'll have for the rest of your life.

Of course, not everything about you is predetermined. Everything is possible and freedom is given. From the moment you stop breastfeeding, you acquire abilities and skills that become part of your personality. Life experiences, difficult and easy, negligible and important, accumulate and leave their mark on you until you are almost complete shaped. It is said that people don't change except as the result of a traumatic event or therapy. I recommend additions and improvements in various forms: professional courses, academic studies, reading and study, spiritual experiences, trips, sports, more and more, everyone according to his own spirit, everything so that at the end, you'll be your own best friend.

That's the goal. I want you to fall in love with yourself. So that you pamper yourself, know how to improve yourself, know how to demand of yourself and forgive yourself. To do all of these things, you need to know who you are. When is the last time you went out with yourself for a meal? I do it a lot. Reserve a table, take a shower, apply face cream, wear cool jeans, a light jacket and that's it – out to dinner. Already in the car I feel great. A meeting with someone I'm crazy about, someone who is just what I need. The hostess says, "Table for one?" I laugh and say "Two."

I order. Start with an aperitif or bottle of wine. Something light, you never know where the evening will go. I'm alone with myself. I don't need to listen, entertain, tell or sit. Nothing. I look at the other diners. In the past, I would have had to spot a pair of diners that I had never seen before. A couple posing as a couple. Today, I use this ability to amuse myself. Who here are lovers? Who left the house with unresolved issues? Who is the businessman with his wife and who is the couple from the office? At the table with two couples, who's with whom? And at what table with two couples is one of the men having an affair with the other man's wife? What do they do for a living? That woman sitting alone, will she eat alone or will someone join her? Will it be a man or a woman? And so on and so forth.

When you're really alone with yourself and you're good, it's unbelievable how people watch you. There are two types of women: those who are interested but have to hide it, and those who want you to see that they are interested. If you really want to know who is interested in you, get up to go to the bathroom, look to the left, and let your pupils go to the right. Let her think that you can't see her. From the corner of your eye you'll see that she is sitting up slightly, examining you and returning quickly to her plate. On your way back from the toilet, make it seem as though you're examining some wine bottle. Again, you'll be able to see how she changes her angle, lifts her chin and examines you. Get it?

It's important that you develop an awareness of feminine nuances. Men make big movements with small results. Women make small movements with big results. There's nothing you can do about it. Just think about how the pelvis moves. It's in their genes.

But I digress.

All in all, I just want to ask you, when was the last time you enjoyed your own company? You must. If you don't enjoy being with yourself, how will others enjoy being with you? By the way, when you're with yourself, you have many opportunities to improve and perfect your style. Learn about wine, talk to the sommelier (wine waiter), ask your server about the dishes, grab something with a complicated name and remember its ingredients.

In order to know yourself, you must first learn about yourself and afterwards, be with yourself. Spend time with yourself, talk with yourself, joke with yourself and philosophize with yourself. You must trust yourself. For this purpose, go out with yourself. This way, you'll have quality time with yourself. Learn new things, examine the world, exploring the small details.

Getting to know yourself is also about developing awareness and recognizing your shortcomings. There is no perfect person. All of us have fears, weaknesses, sensitive points, difficult memories, traumas. All of us are carrying around baggage that affects us negatively in certain situations. What we can do is develop awareness and notice when our genes and character are not working in our favor, to stop for a moment, take a deep breath, and try to change our natural behavior. Remember, at the end of it all, what do we want? That she'll feel and think that you are a good man, a man who knows the street, has wisdom, the heart of a woman and the subtleties that make the difference between "I went out with him yesterday, it was nice," and "Don't ask. We went out yesterday, and I think I'm in love." That's all.

END, FINAL, TERMINAL

....

THE WORLD STANDS AND FALLS
ON THREE TYPES OF SEX

It may seem that dicks have a great life, but they actually have quite a few worries on their head. If I say that sex is everything in life, it may seem a bit exaggerated, but it's not far from reality. Sex is one of the world's driving forces, of man himself and humanity as a society, from the time we started descending from trees and until we began cutting them down.

From Biblical stories, through Greek mythology and to the Internet, sex is the fuel that fires our lives. Devote just one thought to the subject: Spies go through thousands of hours of training on how to take care of themselves and not be caught or trapped. A secret agent learns how to survive in subhuman conditions, eat grasses and snakes, destroy evidence, think ten steps forward, defend himself, stand up to interrogations, trick the most cunning and experienced tricksters, resist temptation, not trust or believe anyone. At the end, why do they fall? Sex.

I personally knew a senior Russian agent. Alexi – the man

and the legend. One of the best intelligence men ever born. A single man who caused tremendous damage to several countries. Cool, bold and clever in ways worthy of admiration. We tried to "remove" him using thousands of different methods, but no luck. In the end he fell. True, this was after an unprecedented investment in building the case. The man had a weakness for Asian women. They knocked him out. You can't ask him any more, but when you have a sexual weakness or fantasy, nothing will help you, especially not us.

The first attraction to someone begins with a sexual signal to the brain. The brain interprets the image conveyed to us by its erotic senses. Relationships rise and fall on these initial sexual connections. The question is not whether the first night was brilliant. The brain is smarter than that. The question is whether the connection awakened something that we cannot live without.

A successful sexual relationship needs two people. I'll talk mostly about your part in it. You have to love. You must love her and yourself. You must love the physicality. You must have desire. The lack of desire in a relationship is a death sentence. The point is that real passion, deep and long-lasting, is not a trivial matter. You need to love your sexuality and hers. You must love your dick and her vagina. You must know to give and how to receive. You must love to give and love to receive. We men love to have orgasms, but you must love the stages before the orgasm. The best sex is when you don't actually want it to end.

Let's first agree on one thing. Not everything suits everyone. Everyone with their own type of sex, and it's just not the same for everyone. Okay? I personally define three types of sex:

Immediate sex.

Existential sex.

Sensational sex.

THE IMMEDIATE

You've been together for a long time. Nighttime, you want a quickie. You love each other, everything's fine. So, a kiss or two, a quick blow job, you go down on her a bit, some missionary-position penetration or a slight variation, a fuck. Orgasm. A hug and a kiss. Love you, good night.

This kind of fuck, from kiss to orgasm, can take anywhere from ten to fifteen minutes. It's a once-a-week type of fuck.

THE EXISTENTIAL

This type of fuck is right for the first night you're together, and also for a couple that's been together for ten years. It's a fuck that understands the yearning for love, touch, attention, warmth, security, giving. It's a fuck that understands that penetration and having an orgasm isn't everything. There are other things, for example, double orgasms. She wants to feel desirable and loved. She wants you to be sensitive and attentive. She wants an embrace. She wants to talk. She does not want distance. You are her man.

This type of sex can begin with kisses, and continue with pampered pleasures like a shoulder rub or foot massage. It can include mutual, slow undressing. There can be candles, music. You can arrange it. Start thinking like a man. It's a fuck with feeling. If there's no feeling, this type of sex cannot exist.

Warm up slowly. Lick her stomach. She bites your earlobes. Pass your tongue lightly over her clitoris, continue on the inside of her groin, she sits on you (without penetration), you caress her chest.

You go down on her. Not for a few seconds, just looking for a way to push in your dick. It's loving, sensitive. Touch her stomach, her calves, the soles of feet. Have fun. Let her go a bit crazy. Turn on your side and lay beside her. She gives you a blow job, you lick her clitoris while she has one foot flat placed on the bed. At the end, you lay her down as both of you want and penetrate.

Don't think about having an orgasm. Remember your friend, your dick. Let him enjoy her vagina. Let your hills rub. Move your dick inside and out a few times. Stop. Rest inside of her. Talk in her ear. Play with the rhythm. Change the angle. Get on your knees. Touch her. At the end, give her everything and tear her up. The final storm, the last, wildest part of the fuck can last between one and five minutes. The fuck itself, from the moment of penetration, lasts anywhere from fifteen minutes to half an hour. Twenty minutes is great. The entire fuck, from the first kiss and until you start trying to get your breathing back to normal, can take between forty-five minutes to two hours. It should happen once a week. Maybe twice, maybe once every two weeks. If you are young or a new couple, three times a week.

THE SENSATIONAL

I'm not telling you to do drugs, but this type of sex requires a rare intensity. A passion that can only be achieved when both people involved are in an ecstasy. This fuck doesn't happen by chance. It happens if you are nymphomaniacs, if you prepare for it as an event, if you're crazy horny, if you use drugs, or everything altogether.

We're talking about a fuck that lasts for a few good hours. It may start at midnight and end with first light of day. It's a once-a-month fuck, or a once-every-four-months fuck, depending on your relationship. It's sex from another world and there is nothing that comes close to it when it comes to strength, experience and release. It's sex for the advanced. Sex that includes games, power, fantasy, perversion. It's free sex, uninhibited and unrestrained. Maximum stimulation that makes the senses crazy. Sex where (almost) anything is possible. Sex where there is more than one hole involved in the game. Including your hole. Including other characters.

If only one of you has experienced this type of sex, the trick is to get the other one to taste from the forbidden fruit. The problem is, comparing this sex to regular sex is like comparing the NBA to neighborhood basketball. One of its advantages is that it is unforgettable, proof of what the two of you are capable of together. One of the disadvantages is that it is likely to become addictive.

With sex like this, it's important that the next morning, or afternoon to be more precise, you share a small coffee together, a smile, an embrace. Otherwise, the memory that stays in your mind is that she's a wild whore. The memory that sticks in her mind is that you're a sadist. Another small problem are the pulled muscles, red knees, stinging crotches, scratches, physical wounds and general exhaustion. But what the fuck.

OMG! I DON'T BELIEVE IT!

....

THERE ARE NO BAD SURPRISES
ONLY BAD SURPRISERS

Women don't like surprises. Yeah, yeah, we heard. That's nonsense. They don't like bad surprises. Just like you. But the element of surprise is great for relationships. The initiative, the thought, the planning and execution are all good and refreshing, not only in themselves but also as evidence of something deeper. There are small surprises that work on nurturing the relationship, and big surprises that uplift the soul. There are surprises that involve large financial investments and surprises that are quite cheap. You can arrange something special for a special event and you can do something simple for no reason at all. The main thing is that it should be surprising and unexpected. The main thing is to stay spontaneous and cool.

1. NIGHT
You get into bed. She folds over the blanket and there's a bra and matching black mesh panties laying on the sheet. There's also a red rose (optional). She tries them on and they fit

perfectly. When did you buy it? How did you know her size? This is the time to tell you that you must know her bra size. Just so you know: a bra has two variables. The first is the body circumference – 70, 75, 80, 85, etc. The second is the size of the breast (the cup) – A, B, C, D, DD, E, etc.

2. TUESDAY

Call her at noon. What are you doing this evening? May I invite you for a drink? An early supper? Yes, even if she's your wife. A little variety. Have an aperitif. Ask how her day was. Tell her an anecdote from the office. Talk about more than current affairs. Dream a little, plan a trip. Eat a bit. Something light. Have another drink. That's all, home. The night is yours.

3. SATURDAY MORNING

She wakes up and goes into the kitchen. Breakfast is on the table. It doesn't have to be caviar and champagne, but it should be a bit special. Toast with blueberry jam, Eggs Benedict, freshly squeezed orange juice, fresh coffee. The smell of indulgence in the air.

4. SUNDAY MORNING

You suggest starting the day at a new coffee shop you've found. Steer the car in a direction she doesn't know. She asks where you're going. We're almost there, you answer. You arrive at the local airport. A young pilot welcomes you. You go to a waiting helicopter. Before she can say she's afraid, you're in the air. A thirty-minute trip. Above the sea, above the neighborhood, above the city, above everything. You land in her parents' town.

They're waiting for you, you told them about the surprise.

5. EVENING
You went to the movies. The cinema is full. The seats next to her and in front of her are empty. She puts her coat on the seat beside her. Remember the tip about the cinema? Five tickets, how much can it cost, really?

6. FRIDAY, MIDDAY
She's at work. The weekend starts in just a few hours. You haven't planned anything special. You call her. Come downstairs, I'm at the front door. You're waiting in the car, along with a couple of friends. She gets in. You drive to a chalet in the mountains, a hotel, a spa, a ski resort. She's elated. After the excitement, she panics; but I don't have anything with me. Everything is fine, you say. Your bag is packed and in the trunk.

7. AT A RESTAURANT
Let's say she was promoted at work or passed an important test. You go to a restaurant. You're seated. You order a bottle of wine. You say to the waiter that she deserves a congratulations because... The waiter nods his head and ushers you to a better table. He leads you to a private room. Ten of your friends have been sitting there for half an hour, slightly drunk. Cheers!

8. THE FRIEND
Moments before the play starts, her good friend who lives far away sits down next to her. How simple, how fun. All it took was five minutes of planning.

9. A MILESTONE BIRTHDAY

Let's say she's thirty. You've been together for three years. You go to the parking garage of your building. Someone is parked in her space. What nerve. She jokes that she wouldn't actually mind having such a car. It's yours, you say, and throw her the keys.

10. TICKETS

Let's say she likes a particular sport or is interested in a specific hobby. Surprise her. Skiing, glaciers, sightseeing tours, a sailing course, a meditation workshop in India, tickets to Beyoncé. So many possibilities.

11. THE PROPOSAL

You're drinking coffee together, looking at the morning paper. A small ad catches her eye. "Dear A. I love you, When will we marry?" It's true her name is Annie, but she really doesn't think the ad is for her. What a cute guy, she says, but how will she know that he means her, she asks. That's what's nice, you say. Slowly, she understands. On the next page, another ad: "It's me, and I meant you." What a guy, she says, admiring the effort. Jealous, you ask. A little, she answers, not really.

And on the next page. "You have nothing to be jealous of, it's me. Want to get married?" She looks at you. Could it be? "Maybe," you say. "Liar," she says, laughing. She turns to the next page. "So, will you think about it? By the way, do you want another coffee?" She's a bit excited now. She quickly turns another page. "We don't have all day. Put your hand in your pocket," says the ad. She hides the ad from you and puts her hand in her pocket. There's a ring. She's crazy about you. Forever.

Let me make something clear. Money helps. But if you don't have any, that's no excuse. We're talking about the idea, not the cost. We're talking about the initiative, the unexpected, the thoughtfulness, originality, grace, humor.

So, what are you planning?

DADDY-O

. . . .

A WORD OR TWO BEFORE
THE BIGGEST STEP IN YOUR LIFE

I'm not pretending to talk about an issue that is so important, essential, and complex as children, in a book that is aimed to nurture you as a man. Still, because I was single for many years and had children at a relatively late age, it seems that I may have a good perspective for sharing with you some thoughts and observations that might make things easier for you before that big step in your life.

The moment you have a child (congratulations!) you're not a couple anymore. You're a threesome. The first child is not an easy test for any relationship. The attention you used to pay each other now goes mostly to the child. Internal balance changes. Your wife, God bless her, may well experience post-partum depression, or simply collapse from exhaustion and stress. You will also have many tasks to complete. In the most difficult moments, remember that this is temporary. Everyone goes through it and at the end, everything works out. There is nothing comparable to the love for a child, and the hard moments are an inseparable part of this love and the journey you go through. As they say, no pain, no gain. Even though you will sometimes feel hopeless to the point of suffocation, you must support your spouse. She needs everything you can give her to go back to being yours, part of the two of you, as before. There are differences in the psychological dynamics between having a son and a daughter. Maybe it's too early to get into it now, but you should know that if it's a daughter, things may be easier on you than on your wife.

In family psychology books, it's customary to define four different relationship axes: father-son, father-daughter, mother-son, mother-daughter. Each axis has its challenges. Before hitting the psychology books, I suggest you read a good book about pregnancy and childbirth. There are plenty to choose from. You don't need to be an expert, but it will equip you with understanding. There is nothing like awareness and knowledge, in general, and especially when it comes to your first child.

Some babies can't fall asleep until you take them out for a drive. The monotonous movement of the car helps them fall asleep. Take advantage of this. Go out with your baby, put them in their car seat, get some fresh air. Stop for a cigarette, look at the sky, take a deep breath and remember that there are thousands of couples who would pay a lot of money to trade places with you.

This is just a sampling of my main advice: Be with your kids. Right away. From the moment they are born. You won't regret it. Touch them. Change their diapers. Bathe them. These activities aren't just for your wife. Take your kids with you. Go for a brisk walk with the stroller. Turn a problem into an opportunity. Children are the longest lasting experience you will ever have in your life. Don't miss out. Your children will be in your image and likeness. They will sense the situation at home much more than you imagine. If your home is filled with joy, love and security, that's how they will go out into the world. The relationship you have with your spouse is the inheritance you leave to them. And what they see is what they internalize. Not what you explain to them. If they see that you respect their mother, they will respect her and their own spouse. You can try to pass on to them your values and beliefs, but all in all, take them as they are. Don't try to change them. You don't have a choice. And anyway, who knows if you're right.

**

Every child has his or her own unique character. You'll see. Let them develop according to their own personality. Don't try to force an egalitarian system and, as a result, erase their private selves. It's true you need to protect them, but you also need to give them space. Let them try, let them fail, let them be burned. That's the only way they'll learn.

Let them be exposed to different areas, for example sports, but don't pressure them. Give them freedom of choice. Don't prove to them that you are a champion because then they won't want to do anything. They won't have a reason to try and be good. Don't give them a reason to give up, because anyway, they don't want to disappoint or be disappointed.

I won't overwhelm you with stories, just one small one. I

took my eldest son to a ski resort. When we came home, I thought to myself proudly how important it was to teach him how to ski. When my wife asked him how it was, he said, "The best part was when I sat with Dad at a coffee shop and we drank hot chocolate and talked about girls." I think I educated him right.

Remember that you're critical of your children because they are you, and you see in them what you dislike about yourself, or what you'd like to be and aren't. When you don't understand their messy room or ridiculous clothes or the awful music they're listening to or their strange hairstyle, try to remember what you thought about your parents when they didn't understand your taste. You thought that they didn't understand anything. It's more important that they talk to you and communicate instead of just doing what you think is right. If they tell you something awful, don't go overboard in your response. Tell them your opinion but don't punish them. Explain to them that the most important thing is that they talk to you, that they don't lie, and that as their father, you will always offer your best advice. Show boundaries. Kids want boundaries. If they don't have boundaries, they go nuts. Don't lecture them about eighty rules you want them to follow. Always talk about one thing.

Here's a small piece of advice: Sunday supper, everyone at the table says something that they liked this week about everyone else at the table, and something that they didn't like. Everyone says something about everyone else. Remember that they see everything about you. Make it legitimate for them to give you criticism. Never ever humiliate them next to their friends. If something doesn't seem right to you, call your child quietly to one side, or talk to them after their friend has left. I think you should aim for them to say: My dad is cool. My dad takes care of me. It doesn't mean that you don't have demands, it just means that you'll also be able to be their friend.

The most important thing – shower them with unconditional love. That's your real legacy.

CODENAME TEHRAN

....

THERE ARE SOME THINGS YOU NEVER FORGET EVEN WHEN YOU GET OLDER

February 2007. I had finished working as an agent years earlier. Steve came by my house. Not everyone has the privilege, but Steve can come any time he wants. Come on, he said quietly. We need your help. Straight and to the point.

The only help anyone needs from an old horse like me is in tests of sustainability. The teams present their plans and I'm supposed to find the holes. Confirm if the risk is reasonable, reject it if it isn't. It's not just percentages and probability. I have always explained right from the beginning that if you throw a baby from one hand to another at a distance of three meters, there's a ninety-nine percent chance that everything will be fine, but the one percent chance of failure can lead to intolerable results.

That same evening, I reported to the office. Our senior agent had been in constant contact with two Iranian generals for more than a year. The hour of truth – the final decision regarding desertion or detachment – had arrived. We had two different sources. Each one had a different thesis. One of them claimed that there were differences of opinion among the generals, even a crisis. Their wives, who had been in close contact, were not speaking. It looked like a black cat had crossed their path, in addition to the affair one of the generals had with a real estate agent.

All night long, we heard summaries from the best people in all areas. Finally, we narrowed down the problem to a single issue: Should we wait or should we activate the plan with only one of them? The benefit: a bird in hand is worth two in the bush. The drawback: the other was likely to discover that he had been abandoned and ruin everything. It was an interesting evening. An evening that demanded imagination, concentration, vision. The decision was made at 4:20 a.m. Presentation of the plan was set for 7:00 p.m.

I stayed at a nearby hotel. I couldn't fall asleep. The knowledge that I was protected and safe while one thousand kilometers away, a drama of life and death was about to unfold, didn't sit well with me. I stayed awake until we were scheduled to present the plan. We decided that the operation would be launched and at the same time, preparations would be completed. In case of a change, there was a point of return. The plan was to remove the general from Tehran in the middle of the night with his family.

We needed forty-eight hours of quiet to implement the plan. Turkey was chosen as the country of transit. "How often do they – the two generals – talk to each other?" I asked. Every few hours. Dave, our director of technology, came into the picture and showed us how we could respond in the general's voice. Unbelievable. The critical hours were the hours of the flight. In the meantime, our plane landed in Istanbul under the guise of a commercial transport plane with less than twelve people on it.

I had Edna. The generation that grew up under me presented a bold and wonderfully creative plan, and with all that, thoughtful and careful. Without egos, dramas or unnecessary risks, and with a deep understanding that this is one operation that cannot be screwed up. Moreover, it would have been possible to save a great deal of effort, but the decision was made that we wouldn't leave any traces. And that already meant challenges that weren't going to be simple.

I approved the operation. Steve smiled in gratitude. Newspaper headlines heralded the disappearance of an Iranian general and his family. The real estate agent also disappeared, as though she had never existed. We had courageous partners, both on the way and in the execution. It all began in a hotel in East Jerusalem. American Colony, American Beauty.

ONE GOOD CORNER

. . . .

IS WORTH ONE THOUSAND STREETS

Your house. We've reached it. Did you think you could avoid it? It's dirty. Don't worry. I'm not talking about the dream home that you're going to buy one day. The mansions of millionaires don't interest me. I'm talking about your house – the condo you bought with great effort, the second-story house with the garden that your parents helped you get. I'm talking about a few basic ideas that will lead you to a better life.

Make an effort to keep one empty corner that is just for you. A desk, dresser, plasma TV and couch. It's your corner. With the empty beer that you drink whenever you want. With the roach of the joint no one else is going to touch.

Where do you read your book? It's best if you have an armchair of your own, and beside it a floor lamp, end table, a few magazines and books. Archie Bunker's chair may well have been a symbol of the chauvinist, primitive man, but every man is entitled to his own chair.

I have a place where I always keep the items I take with me when I leave the house: keys, glasses, mobile phone, wallet, cigar, etc. Everything is always there. Nothing gets lots, nothing to look for.

Your music. It's true that today there are iPods, MP3 players, and the like, but I believe that you need a place where you listen to music. Music is the most universal communication that exists between people, and yet – in my opinion – music is heard alone. Try to have a place like this in your home, with your own sound system, maybe even with vinyl records if that's your style.

Every night, I light candles in the living room and the bedroom. It's fun. Simple and pleasant candles that create a relaxing atmosphere.

Alcohol. Make sure you keep a little bar in the house. Whiskey, vodka, martini, Campari, Pernod, Branca. An ice cube tray, ice cubes, lemon, tonic water, soda water, orange juice, grapefruit juice. What's the big deal? If you have all of those, you're set.

I like wine. I have two wine refrigerators with wonderful wines. To tell you the truth, I love wine so much that I look at the bottles as though they are pictures. Not long ago, we moved into a new house. My wife wanted the refrigerators to be in the garage, next to the washing machine and the dryer. She didn't have a chance to move them. Those bottles are my little chicks. I want them close to me. Keep your little chicks close to you, too.

Books. If it sounds like lip service for the sake of the quality-culture balance, it's only because I don't want to be your education officer. But just so you know, there's nothing like books. Books remind us of the power of imagination and of the single creative person. They show us that the world isn't just a silly TV series and newspaper articles. Collect the good ones, arrange them on some strong shelves and read them whenever you can. The woman who can resist a well-read man has not yet been born.

We've already talked about your bathroom and toiletries, just make sure you keep things orderly, clean, stylish, of high quality and refined. Thick towels, a nice bathroom rug, air fresheners, large, clean mirrors, and cologne bottles. The bathroom is the only place that you and your spouse can feel exactly like superstars. A bit of attention, that's all it takes.

Same for the toilet.

The hideaway. You owe yourself a small area that serves as a hiding place. Not a safety deposit box that can be taken out, but a hiding place. Under the floor, in the wall, a secret passage. Make something up. One day you'll need it.

A fake wallet and keys. Like I said, you'll realize their importance when someone breaks into your house.

Try to cook. It's a great rush. Take a look at the previous chapter on cooking – you'll find a list of products that you need in your pantry.

You don't need to be a handyman, but you should have a toolbox with some basic tools. There are small things you can fix in a minute with a screwdriver. Yes, I know, you're starting to get bored, but there's nothing like a man who can fix the Prada sunglasses that his girlfriend bought for seven hundred euro in Rome. All you did was twist a screw, and she gave you a one-hour body massage.

Between you and me, even if you are in a relationship, don't forget that you are a separate unit. Take care of yourself. Take care of the places that are yours. Preserve the mentality of a lone rider. One day, when you have to ride alone, you'll find that you are already on the horse's back.

The bedroom. You think I forgot?

NIGHTLIFE KING

. . . .

WHEN IT COMES TO THE BEDROOM, DON'T SETTLE FOR LESS

In my opinion, the bedroom is the most important place in the house. No, not just because it's where you fuck (most of the time). This is the room where you meet (night), fall asleep and meet again (morning). Just as you find the bed, literally, that's how you get up in the morning of a new day. Your bedroom needs to smell good, also on a philosophical level. The smell of passion, the smell of adventure, the smell of mystery, the smell of curiosity, and it should smell genuinely good, too.

The bedroom, in my opinion, should be planned and designed so that you can spend time in it before you go to bed. You can make your bedroom a fun place so that your girlfriend won't feel that you are bringing her there just because you are interested in having sex. First of all, make sure that there is a variety of lighting in the room so that it suits different situations. Watching a movie, solving a crossword puzzle, having a conversation, romance, making love, etc. Both dimmers and lamps on the sides of the bed, and a standing lamp. It's not necessary but it is recommended to add a candle or two, also in case of power failure. There are millions of candles and candle holders, and a billion different smells and aromas. Personally, I like candles that smell like the ocean; they aren't too sweet and leave the smell of vacation.

If the space is large enough, add a small table and a couple of small armchairs. That way, you'll create a small sitting area that isn't the bed. On a small bookcase, place books and magazines. There should be a carpet. And pillows. You can start from the floor. I would not install a plasma TV across from the bed, and definitely don't use those ugly wall mounts. What is this – a hospital? Arrange two armchairs, tables for drinks and a screen. She sits, curled up with a blanket watching a show; you lie in bed in your underwear and a T-shirt. Everyone in their own happy place, together. I also recommend a small work area – table, chair, computer. It's nice to be in the bedroom and to do things other than sleep and sex. Imagine that she is on the computer and you show her from behind how to find the address of the hotel in Barcelona.

All of which leaves us with the most important item in the room, the bed. For a third of your life, you're in bed. Sleeping there, loving there, sick there, reading, resting, dreaming, waking up. There's no way you spend more time choosing your living room couch than your bed.

Let's start with the size: I will never understand anyone who lives in a single bed. What is this, a prison? In my opinion, there's only one size of bed – king. People want a big house, a big car, a big fridge, a big room, and on their bed, they compromise. And don't tell me you don't have enough space in the room. There is. I'll compromise on all my other recommendations in exchange for a really good king-size bed. A large bed and mattress is a sign of comfort, space and freedom, and these three elements are guarantors of closeness. It's not by chance that the first thing people say on vacation when they see their hotel room is, "Wow! What a huge bed!" In a king size bed, there is room for everyone: books, a laptop, a child who jumps on the bed in the middle of the night (or woman who wants to suck you off comfortably).

In choosing a mattress, there is only one rule: the best. Only the best. Expensive? Let's do the math: Let's say the best mattress costs four hundred dollars more than the rest. A good mattress lasts for ten years. Forty dollars more a year, three dollars a month, ten cents a night. Five cents per healthy sleep for each of you. To save five cents a night, you're going to live like you're on a camping trip? A good mattress can make all the difference between having a bad sleep and waking up miserable to sleeping like a king and waking up like an angel.

Want to know which company makes the best mattresses? Go to one of the top hotels in your city, tell the concierge that your parents are celebrating their silver wedding anniversary and that you want to reserve the best suite in the hotel for them. Find out about the price and then ask to see the room. In the suite, fold up the edges of the bed sheet and take a look at the mattress manufacturer's name. Tell the concierge you'll think about it for a couple of days and go on your way.

Good night.

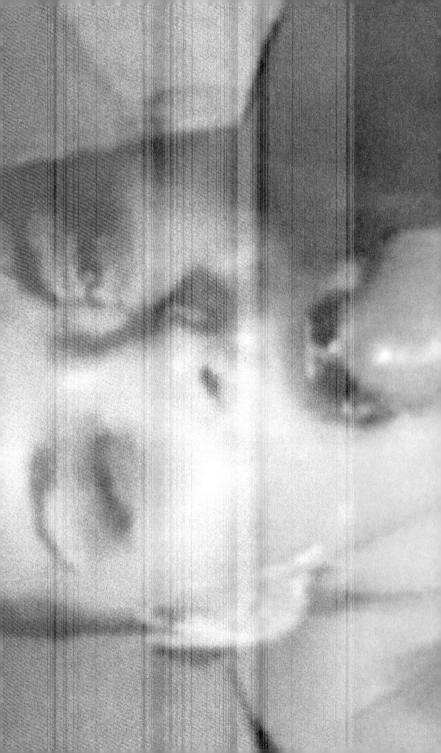

SO, YOU'RE HIS GIRLFRIEND?

....

READ THIS. NO ONE NEEDS TO KNOW

Every man thinks he's getting the perfect blow job. His wife, girlfriend, lover, ex, it doesn't matter. It's good. Lucky for that. Imagine if everyone walked around thinking that outside, there is someone who sucks dick one thousand times better than the person sucking yours. A mess. A big mess. But there's nothing to do about it. Despite endless campaigns to persuade themselves otherwise, it's clear that fifty percent of men haven't yet been able to enjoy the ultimate blow job.

First of all, let's destroy a stupid myth. Many men think that cumming in someone's mouth is a condition for the perfect blow job. Mistake. Mistake with a capital M. Not that I'm against cumming in her mouth. But I cum in her mouth when she doesn't feel like giving me the perfect blow job. I don't complain because she promises that the next time it will be perfect. Every day comes with new hope.

***

The beginning is standard – the mouth on the dick, it goes up, down, licking, sucking and all of that. Already in this early stage, there are those who don't know what they are doing. The mouth is too big on the dick, the mouth isn't tight enough, there's no suction, no pumping. Just the mouth going up and down. Automation. Production line. Why isn't she imagining a chocolate popsicle?

In the second stage, after your dick is wet and you're starting to be happy, she has to work on the top part of it with her hand. Gently but in control. In addition to the movements of going up and down, there's also an art in the circular motion. And there is an understanding that the ultimate pleasure point is one eighth of an inch below the top of the penis. This is the moment when you need to surrender to the touch of magic. The flutter of a determined butterfly.

Then the third stage comes into play: she leans down and starts sucking your balls. She can suck just one of them (if they both aren't clean and fragrant, you'll have to deal with me). Now, we're in a combo movement: the hand moving skillfully on the dick, the mouth wrapping and sucking the balls. Note: she can play with them, eat them or lick them, but in principal, she needs to suck them. And she doesn't just suck them, she sucks them like a baby sucking a nipple. If milk doesn't come out, he's going to be hungry. You can lift your legs to make things easier on her. You can place a pillow underneath. Yes, exactly as you do when you go down on her (you don't go down on her?! Come with me now, we're going to make you familiar with the interrogation room right away).

Now I'm going to share something with you, dear readers.

Right now, while I sit on a Catamaran sailing ship with a bottle of perfect Montrachet, across from the Greek islands, in the final stages of editing, I discovered that my dear publisher removed, right here at the end, a really serious paragraph.

I called him. He says it's too much ("If I wasn't comfortable with what was written, what will the readers say?"). I heard his wife whispering to him on the other end of the phone and understood that on weekends at their place, in Vermont, she'll look at me like a disgusting pervert. I gave up. I guess I'm getting old.

So, just so you know, for the perfect blow job, one thing is still missing. You don't have to compromise. Find it yourself.

YOU CAN'T CHOOSE YOUR FAMILY

A FEW GENERAL RULES FOR RELATIONSHIPS WITH PARENTS ALL FOUR OF THEM

Who am I to tell you how to deal with parents? To this day, I find it difficult to believe that I'm a father. And don't even ask how I behaved with my parents. Aside from that, I have no idea who your parents are, let alone her parents. But there is one thing that all of us have in common: parents are an issue. They pass on to us all of their faults, and want to fix all of their mistakes through us. So I'll tell you a few things, and you decide which ones you want to put into practice.

YOUR PARENTS
Stay in touch with them. Regularity and reciprocity are important. Pick up the phone every couple of days, let them know when you travel.

Don't try to fix them. They're not going to change. Remember what bothers you and try not to be like that yourself.

Take your father out for lunch, go with your mother to a concert. Invite the two of them to supper. In the restaurant, don't run out of patience with them. Have a drink and relax. Be grateful that they have teeth.

Help them as much as you can. Morally, financially, technically. Don't make a big deal out of helping them, don't make a big deal out of it if you can't.

The more the three of you age, don't beat yourself up about things that don't work. There's nothing you can do. Let go of the guilt. The problem itself is enough.

When you're with them, be with them. Don't be silent. Don't get lost in front of the TV. Tell, talk. About everything. Even things that are silly in your opinion.

If they like your spouse, great. If not, don't try all the time to fix it. It's bigger than you are. Don't take sides. They are like grown-up children.

Don't be angry about childhood wrongs. The main thing is awareness. A word is a word. You promise to visit on the weekend – visit. Respect them. For real.

HER PARENTS

In the beginning, her father is your target (after all, you're the man taking his daughter from her current man, which is him). Come in solid, worthy, pleasant. Show him that you respect her. Later, her mother is your main target. Invest in her. She'll take care of everything. She'll show you who your wife is.

Don't agree to arrangements that don't seem right for you from the start. For example, every month at her parents' house. It's possible, but set your limits.

Don't let yourself be bullied. Be nice, considerate, helpful, but don't kiss their ass for some imaginary inheritance.

Don't talk with them about her behind her back. It starts crooked and ends badly.

Invite them to a restaurant once every few months. Every couple of times, invite your parents too.

Don't just show up, eat her mother's food, and then start reading the newspaper. Be present.

Don't take their car. Unless it's forever. And even then, think twice.

Don't work at her father's factory. If you do, you'll end up working for him forever.

Show interest in them. Their relationship with their dear daughter is changing. Right now, they need you. Her father isn't a youngster anymore. Invite him to go fishing, bowling, something.

Give her mother a compliment. Two delighted people at one time.

Try to always listen, maybe you can even get some good advice from them.

Put vodka in their freezer. A single shot will always make your visits easier.

MONOLOGUE FROM THE VAGINA

IF A MAN'S BEST FRIEND IS HIS DICK, THE VAGINA IS HIS SOULMATE

Hey macho, we've talked about your dick, now let's get to know her vagina a bit. For her sake and yours. For the sake of general knowledge, a vagina, like a fingerprint or face, is a unique organ that changes from woman to woman. Every vagina is different from every other one. This has an impact on the right angle for penetration and the preferred position.

There is a lower vagina and an upper vagina (a few centimeters separate the position, whether it is toward the stomach or toward the bottom). There are vaginas that are tight along the entire opening and vaginas that have a wide opening. Labia are the lips on either side of the vagina. Some labia are thin and narrow; others are puffy and fleshy. In some vaginas, the clitoris and labia stick out; in others, these parts are quite hidden. There are smooth vaginas and rough ones. There are short vaginas and long ones. Of course, there are also varying degrees of moisture.

Under strong stimulation conditions, the vagina can expand to surprising dimensions. You just have to get to it, slow-ly. Maybe after she's had an orgasm or two, or maybe when she's really really stimulated. If you invest in the game proper-ly, you'll be surprised by what can fit there (for example, your whole hand).

***

Women who have not experienced multiple orgasms don't like to talk about it. It seems to them like an invention of women's magazines. Well, the multiple orgasm is real. I've checked. I promise.

So what's it all about? There are women, not many (about eight percent), who can have ten orgasms in thirty minutes, all from just finger stimulation. You insert two or three fingers and get them going by moving your fingers in a "come here" type of movement, as though you are scratching their vagina from the inside out. With the other hand, press on the mound of the vagina from the outside toward the inside, and from the top toward the belly button. She can have five or six orgasms this way, and also ten. The more they progress, the more aggressiveness is possible. Three fingers, four fingers, five, in the end, the entire hand. In contrast with women who have trouble having orgasms, the paradox of the multiple orgasm is that the more orgasms you have, the shorter the time between each one. In the end, she can have an orgasm with your dick inside. She'll fall asleep, completely exhausted, but continue to dream about more orgasms. Why is it surprising that some women refuse to believe that there is such a thing?

***

Women who have never experienced female ejaculation (squirting), and we're talking about most women, don't believe it exists either. In the same breath, I can tell you about men who have never had sex with a woman who squirts, and are likely to be alarmed by it the first time it happens. We're talking about women (between five and ten percent) for whom an orgasm can be accompanied by a lot of liquid. It's not funny. We're talking about a quantity that ranges from one to three cups. It's a serious amount that usually ends up on the bed sheets and makes it necessary to change them. This doesn't usually take place during the first orgasm, but the second or third one. Your fingers are inside, there's pressure from the liquid to go out, and your fingers are blocking the opening. Eventually, through the cracks around your fingers, the liquid bursts out like water from a canon. The squirting comes in several waves, accompanying the orgasm. It's a small tsunami, accompanied by groans. Incredible. Even better by adding anal penetration, something which creates an amazing squirting effect, literally like scattered showers. If you're squeamish or scared, don't start with it. If you're an avid lover of sex, it's an experience. Women who are capable of this need an encouraging and active partner, and no – they are embarrassed. The discovery wasn't easy for them at the beginning.

The fluid is not urine and it's not associated with normal discharge. It's a fluid that comes from the womb. It has almost no color or smell. Don't be confused by urination – a "golden shower" – and non-voluntary squirting. To great sex!

THE PEAK OF EXCITEMENT

....

HUMOR IS NOT A SENSE,
IT'S A WAY OF LIFE

Sensitive, spontaneous, funny. It's an old cliché, but it's what everyone wants. Is this you?

It all comes from the same source. The ability not to take yourself seriously all the time, not to always worry what people are going to say about you. The courage to get out of yourself, to tease yourself, mock your own ego and your ridiculousness. Stop for a moment and look in the mirror. Look to the sides. Don't be trapped by conceptions, don't be trapped by paradigms. Only if you can say to yourself: "Who says that…?" "So what if everyone …?" "So what if I had other plans?" Only then will you be able to enjoy the flow of life.

Maybe a better idea came up? Something more exciting? Observation and openness, only they allow feelings to bloom. If you don't let yourself go, you don't feel.

Humor is also the result of observation and openness. Stand-up comedy, usually based on everyday affairs, makes us laugh because it contains everything we know, only from the opposite angle. When you hear a good monologue, you say "Wow, that's right!" and laugh. What's certain is that humor is not about telling jokes. Definitely not boring ones that are badly told. Good jokes are actually stories about life.

A SAMPLE JOKE

A rabbit tells a lion: "I fucked your wife last night." The lion chases the rabbit, the rabbit runs into a pipe and runs out the other side. The lion gets stuck with his head in the pipe. The rabbit runs behind the lion, fucks him in the ass, and says: "Your wife says that's how you like it."

It's a joke, and a crude one, but it's also humor. The fact that animals don't speak isn't relevant, of course. That's how it is in parables. Let's analyze the scene for a moment. The rabbit tells the lion that his wife said that the king of animals himself likes it that way. This may be more sophisticated than you thought at first. Did the lioness mean that the lion likes to fuck her in the ass (and actually hinted to the rabbit that he too could fuck her that way, which means that the woman, that is, the lioness, likes it in the ass), or did she mean that the lion loves when he is fucked in the ass (and in the process, revealed the interesting sex life that she and the lion enjoy)? Or is it possible that the lioness just wanted the rabbit to fuck her in the ass, and the rabbit understood that the lion wanted to be fucked in the ass?

There's one more interesting question. Maybe the joke requires a specific change. The rabbit says to the lion: "I heard that you like to get it in the ass." The insulted lion runs behind him, the rabbit does the trick with the pipe, and when he is fucking the lion in the ass he says: "I swear, when I fucked your wife, she said you liked it in the ass."

In this version, the humor stems from the deep and comic understanding of the lion's situation, in which he must choose between the lesser of two evils: the rabbit's dick in his ass, or the fact that his wife is fucking on the side, and with a rabbit, of all animals. And maybe both. And if the rabbit fucked the lioness in the ass too, then the situation is terrible all around.

And why am I fucking with your brain? So that you understand that humor is observation and sensitivity. If you don't have sensitivity, you won't be able to observe anything in your life. If you don't observe, you won't have a sense of humor. Spontaneity is a type of mental flexibility, anti-fixation and the ability to make decisions on an immediate emotional basis.

We came to all of this from a story. Everything is a story. Like I already said, the world is a stage and life is one big show. Live it. Enjoy it. Not only will she respect you more, but you'll also enjoy life a lot more. She forgot the key to the apartment? Instead of belittling her about how she could lose a key, while waiting hours for a locksmith, get a hotel room, open a bottle of good wine, and tell her about the rabbit and the lion. You may well end up giving the lioness a bit of action in the ass.

BEFORE WE PART WAYS

·······································

SOME PRACTICAL RECOMMENDATIONS FOR IMPLEMENTING THE THEORETICAL KNOWLEDGE YOU'VE ACQUIRED

Every secret agent has been through dozens of courses and training exercises. Creativity and the ability to improvise under pressure are two qualities that are already required in the screening and elimination stages, after which there are many exercises and tests along the way. A trainee who is caught must not talk about his status. Some of the training is to see how he handles things with the police or in prison.

Field agents and collection officers are street animals. They are charismatic and charming, and supposed to have innate persuasion abilities. Go make a nun show you her underwear. A trained agent must not exploit his abilities or use them for evil. I am also forbidden from telling you how to get on a plane without a ticket. But I think I can tell you a few small things that won't harm anyone. Let's just agree that if they catch you, you'll apologize like a man and go home quietly. OK?

***

At every stadium, there's an entrance that leads backstage. Usually, you'll see an equipment truck there. Look for a gray door without a sign. Take a guitar or flute case with you, put an old cap on your head, open the door and go inside, walking with indifference. You're in. Place your equipment in some room and go into the concert hall. Look for an empty seat. Like I said, in the front rows, you'll almost always find empty seats. That's how rich some people are – they don't pay for good seats and don't even show up.

***

At the airport, there are VIP lounges for business and first class passengers. Some people, after they identify themselves and go in, go back outside to do some shopping and return. The attendants at the counter can't remember everyone. Note: Just as you walk inside, turn around and shout to some imaginary figure outside: "Just grabbing the trolley. I'll be right back." Go into the lounge and let the attendant know, with a wink or a few short words that mean, "Hi sweetie, I'm not just coming back, but I'm going out, too." She'll pretend that she remembers you, even though you don't interest her at all. Go into the lounge, no one will look at you. Champagne, salmon, ESPN, a magazine or two, what could be better?

***

It's hot outside. You're bored. Go into the fanciest hotel in the city. Go to the souvenir shop, ask for a large bag with the hotel logo, fill it with newspapers. Go into the bathroom, put on your bathing suit, put your clothes in the big bag. Put on sunglasses, hold the bag in both arms in front of your body, and walk by the concierge straight to the pool. Go into the change room, put your clothes back on, find yourself a lounge chair. A day to relax. Use some creativity to strike up a conversation with some older woman. Invite her for a drink, make sure it evolves into some grilled fish and crème brûlée. Note her key and room number. If she doesn't hurry to sign the bill, sign it with her number. If the mood strikes you, ask her, "my room or yours?" and then take her to bed.

Every bar and restaurant has a back entrance that leads directly to the kitchen. Look for it according to the smokestack, or simply walk along a back alley. Outside the door, grab a greasy tray, walk cross the kitchen and go sit by the bar or at an empty table. You avoided the hostess who would have thrown you out because you didn't reserve a place.

***

A luxury nightclub, just celebrities and models. The city's hottest spot. Dressed in trendy casual, put on some sunglasses. Grab a luxury taxi, preferably a limo. Ask the driver to bring you straight to the door. Give him twenty dollars and ask him to open the car door for you and escort you to the doorman. Now, the dramatic moment. No, he doesn't explain who you are. He tells the doorman that your sister will be there in an hour and he should let her in. Her name is Manissa Johnson. You're inside. Who would dare ask who you are.

***

Night. You and your woman are hungry. Head to one of the more popular hotels and go downstairs to one of the lower levels, where they hold events. There's a sign about a wedding: in the Carousel Hall, Joanna and Joseph Tizi. Take an envelope, put a dollar in it, seal it. Write the couple's name on the outside...You understand the rest, right?

Of course you understood. You've read this far, right? Just remember the tips below are a random collection. Not all of them are applicable everywhere, not all of them are right for you. The important thing is the idea behind them. The accessibility. The protagonist in the middle. You. Trust me, the world is waiting for men that have something to offer. Men who trust themselves, whose senses are sharp and whose charm is obvious. Take advantage of it. Trust yourself. The rest will happen on its own. In your room or hers.

DECENT. COOL. GENEROUS.

....

DON'T LOOK BACK AT THE END, LOOK BACK TODAY. NOW

When you first wanted the girl, the most important thing, the thing for which you lived, was to kiss her. At that moment, you would have given anything you had to make it happen. Tomorrow, when you have something "very very important" to do, don't forget the story of the young girl. For two reasons: First of all, you once wanted to die for someone and now you hardly remember them. Second of all, you kissed her, and more than just one girl.

Time is eternally a true friend. What really matters is not something that you can buy. Money is a limited means of achieving limited, temporary happiness. So what *is* important? Sit on the balcony for a moment, or in the yard, or on the beach. Let yourself fly in your imagination a few years ahead. If this was your last day in the world:

Are you at peace with yourself?

Did you love?

Were you worthy of love?

Were you a decent man? Fair?

Did you give? From yourself, from your abilities, from your possessions?

Were you happy? Did you make others happy?

Have you been a good father to your children?

Did you just pursue and achieve or did you enjoy the way?

Have you left behind, in your image and spirit, something to be remembered?

Not easy, is it?

Now I'll tell you this: we all make mistakes and apply too little and too late what really matters. If you just remember this and implement part of it, you've already done something. After all, it's still not your last day of life. But that day will come. Even if you don't want to think about it. So as Frank Sinatra once said, live every day as if it were your last day, because eventually you'll be right. Be decent, be generous, be cool, funny, sensitive. Try things. Don't be afraid. Of anything. Take care of yourself. Don't get into trouble with the authorities. Your charm won't help you there. The only place where your inner truth doesn't matter is in court.

Take what life has to give you, and know how to give from your life to others. Accept your faults and improve your virtues. Put on sunscreen, leave a big tip. Love yourself. Smile to the world and the world will smile back at you. Maybe not right away. Be patient, attentive, humble. Everyone knows how to talk, listening is much harder. Make room for your feelings. Follow your gut feeling. It hurts you, not the doctor.

You can learn something from everyone. Learn. Know who to get advice from. Let the ego lead you as much as you like, but know how to abandon it in time. A perpetual ego is like a bag of stones you carry on your back. If you've stayed with me till now, you have what it takes.

I think I like you.

Regards to your lady.

Yours,
Mark McCoy

Printed in Great Britain
by Amazon